DEVELOPING A
GENDER POLICY IN
SECONDARY SCHOOLS

DEVELOPING A
GENDER POLICY IN
SECONDARY SCHOOLS
Individuals and Institutions

Jean Rudduck

OPEN UNIVERSITY PRESS
Buckingham • Philadelphia

Open University Press
Celtic Court
22 Ballmoor
Buckingham
MK18 1XW

and
1900 Frost Road, Suite 101
Bristol, PA 19007, USA

First Published 1994

A catalogue record of this book is available from the British Library

Library of Congress Cataloging-in-Publication Data
Rudduck, Jean.
    Developing a gender policy in secondary schools/Jean Rudduck.
        p.   cm.
    Includes bibliographical references and index.
    ISBN 0–335–19153–3   ISBN 0–335–19152–5 (pbk.)
    1. Educational equalization. 2. Sex discrimination in education.
3. Educational equalization. 4. Sexism in education. 5. Women—
Education (Secondary) I. Title.
LC212.8.R83   1993
370.19'345—dc20   93–4049 CIP

Typeset by Colset Pte Ltd, Singapore
Printed in Great Britain by St Edmundsbury Press,
Bury St Edmunds, Suffolk

For my mother, Dorothy

I will have red roses next year. A forest of red roses.
On this rock? In this climate?
I'm telling you stories. Trust me.
     (Jeanette Winterson, 1987, *The Passion*, p. 160)

CONTENTS

ACKNOWLEDGEMENTS

I want to thank the teachers and schools whose work provides the core and continuity of this book. Wherever I went, people were welcoming, open and generous in the time that they gave. Not all the stories that were heard, nor the observations that were made, appear in this book but they have all contributed to my understanding of what the important issues were. I hope that the book will, in some way, strengthen the resolve of those who are engaged on gender work to continue, and encourage others to take their first or second steps. The book is written as a tribute to the vision and determination of those who have struggled on in conditions that were often far from easy.

I also want to thank BP (British Petroleum) for its readiness to fund this research and for its support in making known the achievements of comprehensive schools working on difficult topics in difficult times. In particular, I would like to thank Chris Marsden for his help at the planning stage and Brian Palmer for his help throughout the period of the research.

Thanks also to the many people who offered advice about identifying schools whose practice was worth studying – particularly the advisers and inspectors who talked with me about their experiences of working for equality.

I am particularly grateful to the members of the project's informal 'steering group' who gave up a day of their time at the beginning of the research and again half way through: Lynda Carr, Mairead Dunne, Chris Edwards, Joan Hanson, Mairtin Mac an Ghaill, Isabel Shepherdson, Laura Taggart, Gaby Weiner; Janet Jones representing BP; and also some colleagues from Sheffield University: David Gillborn, Susan Harris and Jon Nixon. Their discussions encouraged me to take a whole-school perspective and to present the data through cases rather than through themes.

I chose to be as responsive as I could, and when the visits and interviews started to expand beyond my capacity to cope I was helped by Susan Harris, who undertook a number of background interviews and observations, and by Laura Taggart who conducted a series of interviews with one of the 'gender leaders'.

I want to thank Rosemary Burnett for agreeing that I could include some extracts from her poetry. And thanks to Brenda Finney, the project secretary, for rescuing me – and the manuscript – from the wilder moments of our new computers.

Finally, I want to acknowledge how much being involved in this study has helped me to understand my own experience, both as a woman and as a woman working in education.

1 INTRODUCTION

Taking a whole-school perspective

Establishing a gender policy for which, and to which, all members of a school are seriously accountable is a formidable undertaking. As innovations go, it must be among the most complex and challenging.

Since the early 1970s we have known about the phenomenon of 'innovation without change' – and the ways in which institutions and individuals seek to protect themselves from disturbance and upheaval. We have seen 'paper innovations', existing only in the words of a document and not engaging profoundly with either thought or practice; innovations permitted to grow only in the walled garden of a particular department's work and unlikely therefore to spread; innovations forced to struggle for survival in the thin soil of marginal activities; and innovations that have clung to their originator and been forgotten when she or he moved on to another school. We have come to realise that innovations that are driven by a set of values and ways of seeing that are fundamentally different from what already exists need, if they are to survive, to be rooted in the deep structures and values of institutional life where they can begin to shape a new logic of practice.

Over the past 15 years or so much has been achieved in schools but by and large gender equality has remained an 'optional innovation' (Acker 1988: 319). The establishing of a common core curriculum was seen by some as a positive step towards ending the differentiation that has disadvantaged girls, but now scepticism is beginning to surface. According to Riddell (1992: 221), 'Some writers have seen the provisions of the national curriculum as heralding a new age of democratic education, whilst others have seen it as even better adapted to serving' – as Arnot (1989) has also said – 'the requirements and the concerns of white middle class boys and men'. Members of the New Right think tanks, which are influential on Government thinking, have offered a mocking hostility, either redefining equality in their own terms or branding it as one expression of the progressive impulse which has, so they suggest, been responsible for a decline in standards.

The Technical and Vocational Initiative (TVEI) has been an important exception to the Government's tentativeness about supporting working on equality issues in schools. A demonstrable commitment to working for equality was a precondition of receiving TVEI funding and also a criterion, built into the monitoring procedures, for the continuation of grants. Many of the accounts of change in this book acknowledge the contribution of TVEI: it legitimated action on equality, provided money to enable first steps to be taken, and established, through its networks, some sense of communal endeavour.

TVEI apart, support for work on equality issues at the school level has in fact come from a variety of different sources within the system (including research and development projects), and the will to continue in the face of predictable setbacks has been sustained largely by the energy of local and regional networks and by the readiness of committed individuals in schools to take on extra work for something they believed was important.

Given the different histories of individual schools, and given the variation in support at the level of LEAs, it is not surprising that schools are at very different stages in their handling of gender concerns. In 1985, according to Patrick Orr, there were still 'large numbers of schools where there is very little understanding of the issues involved' (1985: 21). Very few schools, he added, 'are able to reach towards the ideal situation . . . where work in individual subjects is underpinned by a "whole school policy" for reducing sex differentiation . . .' (p. 20). Progress has been patchy across schools, as Orr points out, but also within schools. Teachers have tended to focus on their bit of the curriculum, and on those aspects of schooling which have been highlighted as a result of the various research and development activities of the 1970s and 1980s: option choices and the images of traditional curriculum subjects; the way that gender is used as a convenient 'marker' or 'divider' in school administration; the differential allocation of teacher time and attention in the classroom; conventional definitions of what counts as knowledge in the curriculum; and the structuring of responsibilities within a school staff. It has been more difficult for schools to get a critical grip on the various ways in which gender underwrites patterns of domination and submission in interpersonal relations.

If ground gained is not to be lost in the face of pressures from a national curriculum which is faint-hearted about equality issues, then attention must now be given to ensuring that gender equality is built into *the structures and everyday relations of schooling*. The aim of the study reported here was to document the experience of schools that were already responding to this agenda – to understand their starting points, the contexts in which they were working, and the problems they encountered on the way.

There are many questions to be explored. For instance, in the absence of major, national reform initiatives that focus directly on gender, how does it get into the school in the first place? Does it strap itself to the underbelly of something familiar and acceptable, or does it enter boldly and without disguise? Who opens the doors? What characterises its passage when members of the senior management team welcome it in and how does it fare when junior teachers are its advocates? In what circumstances is it marginalised? Are conflict and compromise its inevitable companions? What creates the critical moment when individual teachers move from the privacy of committed action in their own classrooms to acknowledge their common concern openly? What external reference points can emerging 'gender leaders' appeal to to legitimise their efforts? What sustains them personally in the face of criticism from their colleagues?

There are also questions to be asked about the notion of 'whole-school' policy and practice. Is it ever an achievable aspiration given the typical diversity of staff and students in a comprehensive school? Is equality a special case which requires that schools try to build a common basis of commitment and a code of conduct that will guide practice? Are there circumstances in which a sympathetic management team would be content with protecting committed action within some curriculum areas and *not* seek to extend that commitment across all staff and all areas of the curriculum?

In one sense it should be easy to manage a whole-school approach to gender in that the evidence of gender inequality is so abundant. One difficulty is that we have become so accustomed to the patterns of gender differentiation and inequality that it is tempting to regard them as 'natural'; as Maxine Greene has said:

> schools seem to resemble natural processes: what happens in them appears to have the sanction of natural law and can no more be questioned or resisted than the law of gravity.
>
> (Greene 1985; in Smyth 1987: 156)

Some teachers (and pupils[1]), thrown by the possibility of a consciousness which calls into question such 'naturalness', try to re-establish the familiar, justifying differences by using the weak but perennially accessible argument of 'biological difference'. The continuing availability of such arguments is testament to the tightness of the patriarchal structuring of perception. However, the 'machine' of patriarchy is no longer as smoothly functioning as it was. The process of questioning is allowing contradictions to surface and is creating spaces where 'constructive educational work' can be carried out in schools (see Kessler et al. 1985: 47).

Gender is a particularly complex issue for schools to handle because its disturbance potential is so high. It disturbs individuals by requiring them to examine their own practices and to acknowledge that they are part of the oppressive structures: they are culpable, they have taken part in 'the continuous creation and recreation of gender differences over time' (Woods 1990: 57):

> to address equality issues is not to deal with external exercises restricted to the realms of the professional or the academic; rather it involves a challenge on a personal level. Confronting equality involves the individual in self examination.
>
> (Skelton and Hanson 1989: 120)

Work on gender equality is likely to surface the contradictions in people's lives, and the compromises which allow us to be governed by one code of conduct in our personal and domestic world and another code of conduct in our professional world. The burden of maintaining this duality on a daily basis is not an easy one to bear – as some of the interviews suggest.

Developing a gender policy 'for which and to which all members of a school are seriously accountable' generally means transforming a collection of *organisationally coordinated* individuals and groups into a body whose *shared values* define the conditions of membership and the integrity of common practice. Such collectivity and coherence of values has not been a striking characteristic of state secondary schooling. In the main it has been the progressive schools, set up outside the state system by committed and often charismatic individuals, which have demanded, and struggled to sustain, collective commitment (Neill's Summerhill, for instance, or the White Lion School).

Some schools have tried to resolve the dilemmas of individual and institutional tension by trying to present equality as a professional 'obligation' – thereby allowing members who are personally uncommitted to live by whatever principles they choose out of school so long as they accept the tenets of the basic code of conduct while they are in school. Such a strategy – although understandable in some ways – symbolically limits the zone of influence of the school to boundaries of its own time and space, and there is no challenge to the divisions and inequities that have cut deep into the structures of the wider society.

Thus, schools that are working out a position on equality face many issues that pull them towards compromise. The business of teaching and learning has to be sustained; a school cannot afford to have waves of aggression and resentment battering at its morale and structures day in and day out. Hence, perhaps, the number of times, throughout the interviews, heads and senior staff talk about the advantages of a 'softly, softly' approach. Even when they are not confronting equality issues, schools are often operating a containment policy: stepping round the edge of arguments, avoiding activating the fuses, concentrating on what Kessler *et al.* refer to as 'well-meaning minor reforms' (1985: 35).

The market situation that schools now find themselves in also urges caution: a school which moves too far ahead of its community with an explicit and emphatic commitment to equality may be taking a risk with recruitment. Such concerns may help to explain why some schools have left the 'dinner ladies', the secretarial staff and the caretaker out of the early phases of review and reform, for they are often the only members of the local community who have daily insider knowledge of the ways of the school and they may be influential ambassadors. Their titles may have changed to 'lunch time supervisors' but only a minority of schools concerned with equality have brought support staff early and fully into their staff training programme.

Moreover, it is not easy, given the segmented nature of schools as organisations, for a head to predict with confidence what the extent of a school's capacity for coherent, consistent action actually is. The greater therefore is the achievement of those heads and teachers who have taken the risk.

The shaping of the research

The research reported in this book was funded by BP as part of an initiative documenting positive approaches to various complex, contemporary concerns in education. I focused on gender in comprehensive schools. Two parallel studies were carried out by my colleagues:

Jon Nixon worked on *Encouraging Learning in Secondary Schools* (forth-coming), and David Gillborn worked on *Rethinking 'Race': The Politics of 'Race' in Education Research, Policy and Practice* (forthcoming). The concern in all three studies was to work with urban or inner city com-prehensive schools.

The first step was to find schools that were reliably judged to be 'doing well' in terms of gender and equal opportunities. I sought suggestions from people who were members of gender networks and who were likely to know the schools in their area well. The people I consulted were very responsive and were particularly enthusiastic about the aspiration to focus on the positive. We talked at some length about the schools that they had in mind so that I could approach those I finally selected with some certainty that their experience was worth documenting.

It was particularly important that other teachers could identify with the participating schools and that the teachers in these schools were confident enough about the progress that they had made to be able to present, without embarrassment or anxiety, the problems that they had encountered on the way. Sugar-coated accounts would be readily dismissed by teachers who are realistic enough to know that there are no easy ways of building gender issues into the core of a school's planning and practice.

At the start of the project (and again towards the end) BP brought together a small number of people who had been actively engaged in work on gender issues: Lynda Carr, Mairead Dunne, Chris Edwards, Joan Hanson, Mairtin Mac an Ghaill, Isabel Shepherdson, Laura Taggart and Gaby Weiner. Two things emerged from their discussion of what a new project on gender should be concerned with. First there was support for the idea of focusing on the structural dimension – the ways in which teachers in different settings are trying to develop a school-wide policy that is designed to influence both perception and practice. Second, there was concern that the study reflect the dilemmas and tensions experienced by individuals and groups who are initiating and trying to sustain the process of change. Both dimensions were reflected in the fieldwork.

In addition to spending time in schools (ten days in the main case study school, up to five days in each of the others) I invited people who expressed interest in the project – or whose work had been described to me – to talk for an hour or more about their experience of work-ing against sexist practices: I also asked them about the origin and development of their own commitment. (Some of this interviewing was undertaken by Susan Harris and Laura Taggart.)

All the interviews were tape-recorded and transcribed and my task was to construct, by selecting and reordering the data, stories or accounts that captured, in a necessarily summary form, the coherence and vividness of the original experiences, their idiosyncracy but also the commonalities that allow readers to see implications for work in their own schools. All the material in the various sections has been read by the individuals or schools that contributed data. In each case, the people most closely concerned had a chance to see how their section sat alongside other sections in the same chapter. No individual or school has been named and all the names that do appear in the text are pseudonyms.

There is sufficient evidence by now to suggest that professionals *can* learn directly from accounts of practice in settings which are similar enough to their own to ensure engagement but different enough to offer new angles and new possibilities for action. Bruner (1986: 4) suggests that such an approach owes much to the way that literature works: 'Characters in stories are said to be compelling by virtue of our capacity for "identification"' or because 'in their ensemble they represent the cast of characters' (the staff of a school, for instance) that readers are familiar with. Teachers who are trying to move forward with their colleagues may take heart from recognising that the snares and setbacks that they are experiencing are not unique to their situation.

The writing-up of the project presented two dilemmas that are worth reflecting on. The first was whether to organise the bulk of the data around themes or around schools. Reynolds and Packer (1992: 176) have argued for more 'good practice' case studies, in which data are 'sliced horizontally' (by school) rather than vertically (by theme) so that a picture of 'school processes in interaction with each other within the school' can be built up and the insights of teachers' collective work can be communicated with due respect for contextual features – actors, time and location. And Hargreaves (1989: 216) has suggested that the picture of comprehensive schools presented through research is often distorted: the literature, he says, 'abounds with studies of poor schools'. I set out, therefore, to produce profiles of positive approaches, at the whole-school level, to the task of developing effective policy and practice on gender equality. The studies of schools are complemented by the stories told by individual teachers who were the 'gender leaders' in their schools.

The second dilemma relates to the project's concern to focus on the positive. We have been weaned on accounts that highlight flaws and failings and that expose the distance between claims and actualities or the differences between teachers' perceptions of how things are and pupils' perceptions of how things are. It is, in fact, more difficult to write engagingly about good practice. I remember reading a review of a biography of George V which commented on the task of presenting the life of a virtuous and well-meaning person in a way that captured and sustained attention. (Milton had similar problems in *Paradise Lost*: Satan is generally seen as a more interesting and more memorable figure than Christ.) But at least with gender there were enough dilemmas and obstacles, enough emotionally charged episodes, to ensure that the narratives had their rocks and hard places; they were not uniformly smooth and green.

Taking some bearings

On 'gender policy'

The term, 'gender policy' appears in the title of the book. My main concern has not, however, been with the drawing up and distribution of written policies for gender equality. Instead it has been with the development of principles that guide practice across schools. In general, the principles, once they are agreed and tried, are formalised in a policy statement, and the policy statement may be used as a way of communicating values and a school code of conduct to pupils and parents; it can thus serve as a way of explaining why particular behaviour leads to reprimands or temporary exclusions.

Teachers are wary of policy statements that are an exercise in tokenism. There is a danger in thinking that once the policy has been approved, gender has 'been done'. But this is not so. Practice has to be monitored and the statement itself may need revising or extending as the school understands better the nature of its own commitment. I vividly remember an MEd student who interviewed a headteacher and asked what the aims of the school were. The head paused, frowned, and said, 'I think they're in the third drawer down', and finally produced a slightly tatty sheet of paper. Hence my caution!

In the final chapter some examples of policy statements are presented and discussed but what matters is the extent to which the principles are understood by all members of the school, and the extent to which they genuinely guide individual and collective practice.

On focusing on gender

I had not anticipated when I started the research that it would be necessary to justify focusing on gender rather than on, say, gender and race. There are arguments in support of both approaches. My reasons were straightforwardly personal: I feel better able to understand issues of gender. Cecile Wright (1987: 184) has said that 'gender variables may operate quite differently in the multi-racial classroom from an all-white classroom' and so, even in schools where there was a substantial number of black pupils I did not feel confident about trying to look at gender and race simultaneously – unless the school concerned was trying to combine the two perspectives. This turned out not to be so, although teachers were aware of the need for such an approach in their work. I think it important to acknowledge this limitation in the focus of the study reported here.

It is also the case that equal opportunities advisors told me that most schools which have not yet started to tackle equality issues at a whole-school level were more likely to start with gender.

Thus, the study concentrated on gender. However, all the schools I worked with were planning to extend (or were already extending) their work to race and disability; by and large class seemed not to be prioritised in the same way.

On focusing on women and men

I set out to record the way that teachers in schools were challenging the traditions and structures that hold disadvantage in place. I was aware at various stages in my own life how the frameworks of public and domestic relations can constrain, exploit and humiliate women. My own sense of frustration and anger peaked, ironically perhaps, after being appointed a female professor in a university where, typically, the ratio of women to men in senior positions was characteristically low. I recognised what Skeggs (1992: 4; drawing on Meis 1983 and on Stanley and Wise 1983) called 'the pathology of the normal', where the norm is constituted by maleness, heterosexuality and whiteness: all these characteristics retain their force 'by being states of unaware-ness, in which the . . . power of the privileged group lies in not noticing their privilege'.

In the schools I worked in, the 'gender leaders' were, in their different ways, seeking to disrupt prevailing notions 'of what is seen to be natural' (Skeggs, referring to Fine and Gordon's work, 1991). They were trying, to use Alison Kelly's words (1985), 'to interrupt the process'; they were struggling to realise an alternative vision.

However, their concerns were not exclusively about transforming the experience of girls. Charged with concern for all their pupils, they also worried about the boys. For instance, they recognised the extent to which some boys were underachieving; they were affected by both class-bound patterns of social injustice and particular structures of masculinity prevalent in their schools or in their communities (see Harris *et al.* 1993). In encouraging debate about gender, most teachers were anxious to avoid a crude and clumsy branding of all boys, all men, as guiltily sexist. An understanding of self in relation to broad structures of socially endorsed injustice has to be carefully developed if boys are to consider the part they might, and perhaps already do, play in the construction of gender relations.

The aspiration of the gender leaders – both female and male – was to help boys extend their range of role models so that neither girls nor boys would see it as unacceptable for boys to acknowledge feelings of sadness, tenderness or fear; or feel humiliated by being short (i.e. shorter than most girls). As Kessler *et al.* have said, reflecting on gender inequalities in Australian schools, 'boys must also be considered important clients for countersexist education'. They went on:

They tend to stay out at present, partly because they are not addressed and partly because they are easily made antagonistic. If, as they are told, women's liberation means women on top, what can it mean for them except the loss of masculinity, which is something they have strenuously been taught to fear?

(1985: 46–7)

Interestingly, most of the boys interviewed in the study were supportive of the idea of equality. The difficulty for them was to hold onto that idea as a principle that might operate consistently across their in-school and out-of-school lives. Kessler *et al.* remind us, importantly, that 'men teachers have a particular responsibility and opportunity here, because what they say and do influences what kind of masculinity is hegemonic in the school'.

On focusing on teachers

In the research, I focused on the experience and perspectives of teachers rather than on pupils because, as Kessler *et al.* have said (1985: 41), in the world of the school '. . . teachers do the main work of maintaining the conservative gender regimes'. But they are also, of course, central to the remaking of gender regimes.

Sandra Acker (1988: 307) has identified three ways in which teachers unwittingly contribute to gender differentiation. First, in a direct way – for example, by treating girls differently from boys and by communicating different expectations of girls and boys. Second, in indirect ways – for example, through the traditional images of masculinity and femininity that are communicated in the habits and structures of institutional life – or, as Jane Kenway and Helen Modra explain it: through the 'various complex and subtle ways in which the different dimensions of schooling are caught up in producing and so reproducing both gender differences and gender inequalities' (1992: 141). And the third way is by failing to take action, even where the structure of the situation is clear and where intervention might reduce bias and disadvantage.

The 'gender leaders' in the case study schools were, in the main, teachers who had stepped back from the comfortable habit of blaming the community or blaming the pupils for 'bringing inequalities into school' – as though schools were neutral sites. They accepted that their schools reflected patriarchal principles: for instance, in relation to the nature of the knowledge that is valued, in relation to ways of responding to indiscipline, or in relation to hierarchical structures. They set out to work with their fellow teachers and they sustained their efforts to bring about change during a period of considerable controversy and strain in education – at a time when it would have been easy to give in or give up.

On the language of 'equal opportunities'

I should also explain that in writing from the experience of schools the language of 'equal opportunities' is often used a language which has, in recent years, been criticised for embodying, ultimately, a spirit of compromise rather than challenge. As Arnot has said (1992: 44): 'The version of social equality being used emphasised equality of access rather than equality of outcome – a much weaker version than some would wish' in that the fundamental structures and divisions are not being taken apart; rather, space for 'the disadvantaged' is found within them. Indeed, Madeleine Arnot (1992, discussing Elizabeth Wilson's work, 1980) has argued that 'women's oppression' has not only not been visible but that 'women have been silenced by the ideology of equality of opportunity'. Sheila Riddell, in her book *Gender and the Politics of the Curriculum* (1992: 213), endorses this view, suggesting that some equal opportunities campaigns 'have operated on the rather simplistic expectation that all that needs to be done to achieve equality is to enlist females in traditionally male areas of the curriculum and the labour market without altering subject content or occupational structure and ethos'. And Sandra Acker (1988: 312) contributes the observation that while 'forcefully feminist' approaches tend to make teachers wary (she cites Ball 1987 and Whyte 1986), this is not to argue that radical feminist ideas should be disguised in equal opportunities clothing; what it indicates is 'the possibility that social acceptance has not progressed sufficiently in Britain to allow schools to move smoothly in that direction'. The data from the study reported here tends to confirm this analysis.

Overall, I think Kessler *et al.* strike the right balance when they say that 'we must find ways of talking about large-scale structures without reifying (them) and about personal practices without losing their large-scale contexts' (1985: 35).

On writing for a teacher audience

This book is written for teachers as a way of sharing ideas and experiences across different school settings. I have chosen to use a direct, quasi-narrative style for presenting the data – largely through preference but I also have the following words echoing in my mind:

> If intellectuals have to talk to each other in specialised terms, so be it. The question becomes, 'Does that get translated at some level into the classroom?'
> (Lentricchie, quoted by Lather 1992: 122)

In the case of gender, the intellectuals and the practitioners are often one and the same, but the concern remains not to disregard the classroom and the school for these are the arenas for action that can help transform practice.

In reflecting on the data, across individuals and across schools, I have drawn extensively on the thinking and analysis of others who are concerned with gender. I wanted to maximise the accessibility of the text while offering, through the references, signposts – for those who want to follow them – to further reflection and debate.

Focus of the chapters

Chapter 2 presents very short pieces from a series of 'biographical' interviews where both female and male teachers reflect on the episodes and incidents in their lives that led them to take action or support action on gender equality in their schools.

Chapter 3 presents four short narratives of the experiences of 'gender leaders' who were seeking change in their schools. The narratives are edited from interviews with three women and one man: three were members of the senior management team (one head and two deputies) and one was operating from outside the senior management team. In one narrative the speaker looks across 12 years of work on gender equality in his school; the other three present the speaker's experiences over the last few years – sometimes as a 'first attempt' to tackle equality issues and sometimes as a second attempt after an earlier initiative in the school had lost impetus and faded.

Chapter 4 presents accounts of progress in three different school settings. The growth points in each school are different: in one, work on gender started in drama and spread through the curriculum; in another the work focused on measurable outcomes as representing a professionally acceptable way of ensuring that staff took responsibility for looking at gender differences; in the third, International Women's Day was used as a publicly legitimised way of getting into work on gender.

Chapter 5 offers an extended account of the progress made in one school over a three-year period. The senior management team pushed the boat out and kept it moving, with determination and skill, despite constantly choppy waters and, at times, waves high enough to turn less committed travellers back to the familiar harbour that they had started from.

Chapters 6 and 7 draw together the experiences of the various stories and accounts presented in the earlier chapters and consider how such achievements should be judged. The task of evaluating progress is complicated by the depth of the contradictions that individuals and groups experience in relation to gender equality, and by the consequent prevalence of responses that exhibit, simultaneously, both accommodation and resistance.

The chapters are sequenced to move from the nature of individual commitment through to the problematics of achieving institutional commitment. Despite the differences in setting, there are common experiences and common themes across the various stories and accounts. As the reader moves through the chapters, the hope is that understanding will be cumulative – in much the same way that life experience is for John Berger:

the road already travelled curls up behind us, rolls up like a film. So that when [we] come to the end, [we] discover that

[we] carry, stuck there on [our] back, the entire roll of the life that [we] led.

(1992: 58; quoting Ortega y Gasset 1984: 187)

Note

1 In this chapter and in all others, the word 'pupil' is used rather than the word 'student'. The schools differed in their terminology but 'pupil' was still the more common.

2 INDIVIDUALS AND THEIR COMMITMENT TO GENDER EQUALITY

> As teachers we need to reach into our own histories and attempt
> to understand how issues of class, culture, gender and race have
> left their imprint upon how we act.
>
> (Giroux 1983: 241)

It would be difficult to find a school at the moment where equality
was so firmly built into the texture of everyday relationships, aspirations
and patterns of achievement that there was no need of any special
impetus or review. Although 'equal opportunities' has been an important strand of TVEI activity, there have been no major national
projects that have been designed to effect whole-school change. In the
main, the development of equality issues has needed the energy and
patience of committed individuals who have led and sustained school-
focused – not just subject-focused – initiatives. Such individuals have
often used external programmes, events or slogans as a justification
for getting things going in their own institutions but they are invariably
fired by strong personal commitment.

In the participating schools, the commitment of the women gender
leaders seems to have come in the main from reflection on their own
experience, whether as child, partner or teacher. Here are some brief
accounts of the moments of realisation which are seen, retrospectively,
to have been important in constructing individual commitment to
action in their schools.

Ann

I think I first became aware of inequality when I was taking a break from
work and became 'the wife' of a man at work and began to encounter

questions at the door such as 'Is your husband in?' or, at parties, 'What does your husband do?'. And when I returned to work after a break I began to see, in my coeducational comprehensive school, features of bias and inequality which had not appeared in my early teaching experience which had been in a girls' school. Although I had had a promoted post after one year in my first job, when I returned to teaching I had to return as a scale 1 teacher in order to get a job. Although I was quickly promoted again I discovered that this was a pattern in teaching.

I observed that in schools which had become larger as they became comprehensive the management structure was overwhelmingly masculine. And when I myself was promoted to a middle management post and therefore became part of a head's policy team I found that the ethos and the behaviour and attitudes of that team, its jokes, its manner of talk, were overwhelmingly male. I also noticed bias in careers counselling, bias in the choice of subjects, and a lack of seriousness in dealing with harassment of girls. I also noticed young male teachers (I was then in my mid-30s) being advanced up the fast track beside me when able women were doing a great deal of the work of the school on low pay.

When I began to apply for promoted posts, at my first deputy headship interview in 1980 I was asked by the chair of governors of the school, 'You're a single parent (I was by then separated) and you have two children. You already have a busy job. If you had this job would you have time to spend with your family as well?' And I was asked in subsequent deputy head interviews, or in private interviews during the day leading up to the formal interview, a series of improper questions about my personal life as a woman and a single parent: for example, I've been asked whether I intended to marry again.

Well, naturally, I became very interested in equal opportunities at this point, from my own experience as well as what I was observing. Also, as a parent of two sons, I became increasingly aware of the natural way in which they went into a range of opportunities in life, particularly outdoor sports, canoeing, climbing, camping, without fear and with the expectation that they would achieve. And as they grew older their expectations of higher education and of a serious career with a good job were very secure. Watching my sons I could see the way they claimed educational opportunity. This was a lesson to me too.

Briony

My first teaching post was in a boys' school. It had been a boys' grammar school and it was still run on fairly traditional lines. Rugby and sport and rowing, all these sorts of things were very important. But it was my personal experience as a very young female member of staff in a staff that was predominantly male that hit me very hard. There were a few older women and two who were married. I was the only single woman on the staff. I felt very much a victim, if you know what I mean. The men would make comments about my clothes, for instance. I used to wear a lot of scarves so they had this little joke, asking me which airline I was working for today, and things like that. It was very cold in winter once and somebody said, in front of all the other members of staff, 'It's cold so I'm just going to stand close to Briony and warm up'. I felt powerless. I thought, well, there's no point getting upset but I don't like it and they shouldn't be doing this, and why should the fact that I'm a woman matter.

And it was particularly annoying that they asked me to be the minuting secretary for the heads of department meetings. Now that's when I really started to feel it because there were no heads of department who were women and I was the first woman to go into this male meeting apart from the secretaries who brought the tea. I actually felt quite important hearing it all – but I was in a servile role. And what was I supposed to do? I wasn't a head of department. I didn't have a voice. I wasn't supposed to say anything because I was a minuting secretary. I wasn't there to say anything and yet I had to take this kind of comment. So I started to think how to deal with people who were doing this to me. I couldn't get aggressive because I thought they'd only retaliate and do it the more.

All these experiences, I think, made me really question the role of men and women and their attitudes to each other. But as gradually more women came onto the staff and became concerned about it, I felt a bit stronger. That school was so very male in its ethos, among both the staff and the boys. I thought that something ought to be done about it. As an English teacher I felt that this macho force that was driving through the school made it difficult for me to encourage sensitivity among boys. By the third year you had to be tough, and if children didn't develop this toughness they often became victims.

In the end I actually asked for it to be brought up as an item on the agenda at a staff meeting and I prepared a paper. I'd been there about three years by this time and I must have felt there was some support and interest among the women staff, and, importantly, from the male head of English. So it wasn't just me saying something. Anyway I prepared this paper and said I was concerned that we were creating boys to be men in a very traditional sense, and that the world that they were going into wasn't going to be like that. As future fathers they would be expected to share equal roles with women. I said I was worried because we were not opening their minds to alternatives, or allowing them to be sensitive, or to take a passive role in a relationship, or just generally think about themselves as not being the big tough guys that have to go out and hunt the meat.

My paper was received politely but I remember one person saying to me afterwards, 'I do agree with a lot of the things you said but, you know, you won't change things'.

Carrie

I think the route into gender for me was through deep personal frustration in my marriage and the lack of emotional intimacy. I went for help, I read and ultimately I came into 're-evaluation counselling'. Through that I found that there were men who were willing to address their own sexism. And when I came back into teaching full time I realised that what I'd actually needed was what I'd gained in the end mainly through my own efforts, my own personal journey, struggling to make sense of being a wife and mother as well as a person. And I'm committed to trying to enable others.

I started teaching in a girls' grammar school and I only grew as a teacher when I came into comprehensive teaching – when I came to this school really. I suppose I've come to understand that what I'm really about as a person and as a teacher is the persistent pursuit of relationships that are based upon respect. You know, that's the only way. There isn't any other way that I know of.

The passage between personal and professional life, the readiness to look across from one to the other, is what helps sustain Di's commitment. Her strong support for women grew out of her personal experience and is sustained, in part, by her awareness of the struggle that women often experience in carrying their values through into their professional worlds and, at the same time, reflecting those same values in their private lives.

Di

I am almost afraid that even though I have this awareness myself I might not act on it with my own boys. I have a very good friend, Jane, who has two daughters, eldest and youngest, and a boy, Seb, in the middle. She is very happily married but we have similar views on the kind of wimpishness of a lot of men who need this other person to prop them up. She would say, 'We do it to our boys' and I would say, 'Oh, no I don't' and she would say, 'You do. I have seen you with Jack' – Jack is my little one. Even though he is five, I should expect him to do more and I am still making excuses – okay, there is only me with them. They see their dad quite often and we are friends again, but they see me doing all the domestic things. Sometimes I don't make them clean their bedrooms or wash the pots up or whatever. Jane would say the same of her girls. They are 'naturally' interested in domesticity. Seb couldn't give a bugger about it and for the sake of a quiet life she does a lot more for him than she does for the girls and yet we are two women who are aware. That disappoints me, that we ourselves are still wrapped into all this, whatever awareness we have got.

The male gender leaders in the participating schools (those that I interviewed were all white heterosexual males) were more likely to have been influenced by concern for the life chances of their partners, by their partner's own commitment to equality issues, or by a sense of unease about conventional masculinity. Connell (1987; 1991: ix) points out that 'where men in general are advantaged by current social structure', commitment to equality can mean 'costs for men in their social advantages, sometimes serious ones'. But, he goes on, 'there are some groups of men who can recognise injustice when they see it and are far from comfortable with the position they have inherited'. Connell offers five reasons why some men are prepared to support the fight for equality:

- Even the beneficiaries of an oppressive system can come to see its oppressiveness.
- Heterosexual men are often committed in important ways to women . . . and may desire better lives for them.
- Heterosexual men are not all the same or all united, and many do suffer some injury from the present system.
- Change in gender relations is happening anyway . . . A good many heterosexual men recognise that they cannot cling to the past and want some new directions.
- Heterosexual men are not excluded from the basic human capacity to share experiences, feelings and hopes. This ability is often blunted, but the capacity for caring and identification is not necessarily killed.

(1987: xiii)

These perspectives were reflected in the stories told by the male teachers who were actively supporting equality in their schools, including gender equality.

Alan

I've always read widely in terms of politics and particularly sexual politics. The sort of stuff that came out in the 1960s and 1970s was of great interest to me. I am married to a feminist who is a solicitor and very successful. I have always supported equality of opportunity in schools and education and I feel actually free to do things that are non-traditional. You know there's something in it for me here. I am more able to express my feelings, I am more able to say 'I feel terrible', I am more able to question macho male behaviour. So for me it's actually to do with my personal history but it's also very deep, developmentally, for me as a person, as a man in this very male dominated society. I'm a white middle class man in this society and I can actually say, 'Well, I don't want to be in that particular box'.

When I arrived here there was a totally male management team and having always had an interest in equal opportunities and gender and the politics of feminism and these sorts of things I found it rather disconcerting to move into this all-male atmosphere which pervaded the top management of a mixed comprehensive. There was very little I could do as a new deputy and the head at that time was quite threatened by strong women. I used to run a disruptive centre before I came here and the girls who came to it I thought were very interesting because some of the things they had done, like telling a teacher to fuck off or striking somebody or something like that, I wondered if they had been boys whether they would have gone so quickly through the process of getting to a disruptive centre. The other thing I wondered was whether these girls, these young women, had looked about them, seen the inequality about them and got very angry about it and saw that they were treated differently from the boys. They were perhaps not very articulate and were perhaps from a background where this sort of male domination was reinforced. Their anger was pretty ill-expressed but it came out as anger.

As teachers we have to look at what we are doing, at what is happening to young people. I believe that people develop and grow the whole of the time they are actually being forced to re-evaluate and question.

Barry's story was less about gender or race as specific arenas for action and more about a broad commitment to equality as a principle for handling inter-personal relationships.

Barry

I went to an all-boys' school. I worked in a department in the University that was exclusively male and I worked in an all male industry. Having said that, I felt as aware as a man possibly could be of gender issues. My partner had a big influence on my attitudes and she has been involved professionally with equal opportunities issues and both gender and race at a national level. So I felt I had an understanding of what the issues were. I might be aware of the issues, but it doesn't make me perfect in what I do all the time.

I can explain it best if I go back to think of what happened when I was in industry. I was trained as a mining engineer and I went into mine management. In the late 1970s, early 1980s, I was a bit of a high flyer; I got a lot of promotion and benefitted from management training courses. The job involved motivating people, negotiating joint objectives, using a conciliatory approach to union relations and so on. Then, after the miners' strike, the style of management changed which is why I ended up getting out because

I didn't want to manage using the threat of redundancy or the carrot of bigger bonuses . . . you can get short-term results that way but in the long term you lose things like respect and credibility. Now in schools I see exactly the same parallels. Here, I am allowed to operate how I used to operate before the strike in industry.

Barry recalls his response to the advertisement for the post at his school:

There were words like equal opportunities, gender, race, responsibility, sharing, respect. They were also highlighted in the interview and that made me think that this is a worthwhile place to teach . . . When you get to the school you realise that policies are being practised. We feel we can make it happen.

He goes on to explain how he tries to avoid macho models of control that are still prevalent in many schools – an issue which Alan had also talked about. Both teachers were aware of their own vulnerability in abandoning the conventional strategies which allow men to exert control and to win the respect of young men and, often, of fellow teachers:

In school I have a great reluctance to shout. It is not me imposing my voice because I am bigger and I am the teacher and I am the boss and I am going to put you down. It is not that. Now I would be less than honest if I said that never happens, because we are human. I virtually always apologise to students if I do shout. After I have cooled down I say, 'Sorry I shouted then, but you could see how you were winding me up' and we go through why I shouted and what should be done about it. I have shouted at a whole class but that is even less effective and I have lost my temper with a whole class and I have had to say, 'Look, you have got me losing my temper. This isn't the way it is going to be' and we have talked that through.

Christopher's account, like Barry's – and indeed like Briony's – focuses on the rejection of the macho culture of the all-male institution.

Christopher

How did I become committed to equal opportunities? Well, there was no discussion of gender on my PGCE course – where I was a mature student – but I did my major block teaching practice at a comprehensive school on a massive sprawling council housing estate and it was all boys and there were 1800 of them. That was a culture shock because I'd never worked in that sort of environment before. Most of the staff were men. Having 1800 boys in one institution was very strange and so it became an issue for me – the unfamiliarity, the ludicrousness and the problems it created. I'd been to a coeducational school myself. Before going into teaching I'd run courses in industry, always for mixed gender groups, so suddenly finding myself in an all-male setting was very strange. I think it focused my attention on boys' behaviour particularly, because it was so much more extreme in the boys' only situation. I think I was probably making comparisons between my own education and what I was seeing. It certainly focused attention on the macho attitudes and the aggressiveness of boys, and their dominance.

And then a strong influence was working under a particular head who was very principled and whilst gender wasn't an up-front issue in the way it's been in my present school, I learned the importance of having a code of conduct that embraced many aspects of school activities and relationships. And when I first came here I was struck by the macho behaviour, the aggressiveness, the violence. I suppose I'm mentioning violence because at heart I'm a pacifist. So violence at one end of the spectrum might mean shouting at kids and at the other end of the spectrum might mean physical aggression and obviously it impinges on the gender issue in particular in terms of male attitudes towards women.

In rejecting the licence to dominate that characterised the environments that they had worked in, these male teachers were not supporting the circumscribed view of female presence as a gentling and civilising influence: in each case, the concern was for interactions that are founded on respect rather than on the assumed privilege of power.

Comment

> Having made a discovery I shall never see the world again as before. My eyes have become different; I have made myself into a person seeing and thinking differently.
>
> (Polanyi 1958: 143)

There are two recurrent themes in this book. One is the relationship between individuals and institutions; the other is the relationship between the 'landscape of consciousness' and the 'landscape of action' (Bruner 1986; in Rudduck 1991: 95–7). The teachers quoted above were all, from their different positions in schools, intent on moving through the landscape of consciousness – where events and encounters in their own personal and professional lives had led them to reflect on and clarify their own values and concerns – to the landscape of action where they were helping colleagues to dismantle the structures that generate and sustain inequality. Interestingly, 'individuality' in teaching has often been used as a metaphor for privacy, but in work on gender, the individual's sense of injustice – whether experienced or observed – is an effective starting point for action with and for others.

The teachers quoted above understood the need for change in themselves and in the system. The challenge for them is to help their colleagues. As Jennifer Nias has said (1984: 14), many of the profession seem to receive little real help in working out their own values. Significant change will not be achieved by teachers who feel caught up in proposals for change that are always someone else's idea. They need to feel some sense of control over their own personal and professional worlds – even while they are in a state of flux. Without some sense of 'hurting' because of the way things are, teachers may feel that they are too closely implicated in past perspectives and present practices to contemplate change. To feel in control may mean finding some way of identifying with a particular proposal for change and making a personal investment.

In short, development in schools is, I think, likely to be more powerful in its engagement with fundamental issues if teachers have constructed their own narratives of the need for change.

3 GENDER LEADERS IN ACTION

Tackling gender issues in an explicit way and on a whole-school basis is no easy task. It takes commitment. Status in the school hierarchy helps; it can endorse the individual's right to initiate consultation and action and to monitor progress, but it offers no automatic protection from hostility.

The task is difficult in a number of ways. First, even in educational settings which have long espoused the principle that their business is to help every individual fulfil her or his potential, that principle usually guides practice in an incomplete way; its meaning has been constructed within a framework where the prevailing notion of equality is limited by the patriarchal structures that shape our ways of thinking and relating so profoundly that it is difficult for any of us to peel away the layers of assumption and to 'see' things differently. There can also be a problem of 'benign apathy': it is unlikely that anyone working in a school would be 'against' equality but those who know from experience, or who see through reasoned analysis, what equality could and should mean in practice are still in a minority in many schools.

Second, we are all obliged by the multiple demands of our working lives to consign some of our activities to routine: habit is comfortable and anxiety-free. It is therefore disturbing to change our routines, especially when, as with gender, the values that underpin those routines network our behaviour with a robust continuity. It is like trying to clear a garden of nettles – the complexity of the underground growth system is formidable. Pulling up a few plants may look better, but it is not doing any long-term good. The problem with gender is whether you concentrate on removing some of the more obvious inequities or whether you aim ultimately to tackle the root system. Gender leaders in schools tend to travel optimistically; and often the complexity of the task they have taken on only reveals itself gradually. Their personal commitment, along with some sense of progress and a feeling of growing understanding and support among colleagues, will help to sustain the action when the going gets rough.

Third, working on equality issues almost invariably proves to be divisive, and often uncomfortably so. The diversity of people and perspectives that make up a school staff is not often exposed. The degree of consensus at the level of values is not often tested. As Giroux (1983: 96–7) points out, 'the relationship between the dominant school culture and the contradictory, lived experiences that mediate the texture of school life' is interestingly complex: whatever the assumed force of the public policy agreements, there has, in the past, always been the refuge of one's classroom where the teacher can be her or himself. As Huberman's 1989 study pointed out, teachers who have the greatest satisfaction in their working lives are those who have avoided major innovation: they were involved (to use Huberman's metaphor) not in land reform but in tending their own window boxes, actively and regularly making small improvements – changing texts, experimenting a bit with pedagogy, trying out different ways of engaging interest at the start of lessons. But equality, for most schools, does mean land reform – and, more than that, it is difficult to avoid, at some stage and at some level, the serious re-examination of self.

One of the four stories that follow is told from the perspective of a teacher, Kate, who is operating from a position of some authority but outside the senior management team. Deeply committed to equality issues, she was able, in her new post as TVEI coordinator, to build up widespread support for equality in unobtrusive ways while giving attention to information technology – the TVEI priority that her head wanted her to focus on. The other three stories are told from the perspective of members of the senior management team who, when they joined their schools (Fran and Emma as deputies, Geoff as head) made gender equality a priority for the school. In each case, they were supported by other members of the senior management teams and by individual teachers who, while sympathetic to equal opportunities, had not yet tried to coordinate activity at a whole-school level. In the late 1980s, when Fran and Emma took up their new posts, TVEI had put gender on the national agenda, but when Geoff became head in the late 1970s external support networks for gender were less developed and it was more difficult, in some areas, to find external sources of money to pay for cover and to back in-school initiatives.

The four schools all served white working class communities in the Midlands/North of England but the profiles of the schools were different. Kate's school is a large 13–18 comprehensive, on the outskirts of a city, with open countryside beyond. It serves a socially mixed community: pupils come from council estates, from some modern privately developed housing estates and also from some established middle class areas. The school is part of a modern complex with a sports centre.

While Fran's school had a working class core, new local building programmes and rehousing schemes gave it both a proportion of middle class pupils (about 15 per cent) and a substantial number of pupils from highly disadvantaged homes. One of the school's curriculum strengths was its commitment to discussion-based learning, particularly in the humanities area, and there were also existing pockets of commitment to equal opportunities. When Fran arrived, her aspiration was to extend that commitment across all departments and all areas of school life.

Both Fran and Kate start their stories by looking back at their experience of gender issues at their last schools. Fran was a somewhat hesitant onlooker while Kate was an enthusiastic initiator. Both learned from these experiences, and the learning informed the approaches they took in their new schools.

Emma's school is located in an urban area; over the years it had built trust among its solidly traditional working class parents through offering a secure, unfrightening familiarity. It had a good reputation and pupils were generally well-behaved. The last head was long-serving and had acted very much as the *pater familias* both in and outside the school. The new head and Emma, the new deputy, offered staff more opportunities for participation and consultation in decision-making, which they wanted, and tried to change parts of the established order while retaining the support of their community.

Geoff's school is out of town, with fields nearby, but has many of the characteristics of an inner city school in terms of levels of disadvantage and high unemployment. It serves an ex-mining community. Geoff had joined the school at the time when it was changing from a secondary modern to a comprehensive. Change was expected and he steered and sustained a radical course, including a policy of no uniform and the employment – in an all-white school serving an all-white community – of some black teachers. He managed to build up a strongly supportive staff. The school continued to be seen as somewhat strange (i.e. radical) by its feeder schools but it was the community school and parents sent their children to it. If, in the 1990s, market forces encourage this white working class community to see choice of school as problematic, then traditionalism may prevail and the school may have to face either losing some students or compromising on some of the educational principles which have served its pupils well in the past.

In all four schools – which had no, or only very few, black pupils – there was concern at the high level of racism in the communities. Each school was involved in introducing some work on race but the stories that follow focus on work on gender, which is where the initiators chose to start.

The four stories were edited down from transcripts of long interviews (or, in the case of Kate's story, from a series of interviews). Early drafts and the final versions were cleared with the interviewees who also saw their own stories in the context of the other material in this chapter.

The stories offer the perspectives of the initiators. Data gathered from other sources (staff and pupils in the schools; documents etc.) suggest that the stories are factually reliable but the emotional colouring reflects the highs and lows of the individuals who were taking the initiative, their sense of isolation at times, their pain and frustration, their excitements, and the way they developed strategy out of reflection on experience.

We start with Geoff's story which is an overview of 12 years of sustained commitment to equality; next come Emma and Fran's stories which cover the first two to three years of coordinated activity in their schools; the chapter ends with Kate's story which looks back on a year's work in one school, two years' work in another – and looks forward to the challenges of a new post in a third school.

Geoff's story

When I first joined the school I was appalled by the way boys treated girls and I was appalled by the way male staff treated female staff. I was appalled by the way fathers treated wives, fathers treated daughters – by the way that men dominated women.

I can remember almost word for word the first meeting I ever had with a parent in this office. It was about a boy who'd been disruptive and I'd written to his parents to say I'd like them to come into school to meet me to discuss their son's behaviour. Well, the father came and we had quite a useful exchange and as he was leaving he said, 'Well, thanks very much for seeing me and let me know if my son's a problem again in future'. And I said, 'If anything crops up at home or you don't feel happy with the situation, please don't hesitate, both you and your wife, to contact me. It will be nice to meet your wife as well'. Obviously I'd said something that he didn't like and he wheeled – he'd been very civilized up to then – and he wheeled round on me and said, 'I'm in charge of our family' – and he left. Now that was my very first sort of official meeting if you like in the role of head with a parent and I shall never forget it. Others weren't quite as outspoken as that in terms of making their attitudes clear.

Then there was the fighting. I can remember vividly the first fight I experienced here. It took place just after the end of school and I was working in the office and all of a sudden there was a mass of kids charging past my window. I was bemused. I thought where the hell are they going and then, about a minute later, a member of staff charged into my office and said there's a horrendous fight on the field. So I ran to the field, collecting two or three members of staff on the way, and when we got there – and this is not an exaggeration – there must have been two or three hundred students, mainly boys, and they were in a big circle, linking arms and preventing anybody getting through. In the middle were two girls, fighting. They were fighting, as I later discovered, over a boy. It was like cock-fighting, you know, bear-baiting. It took three of us two or three minutes to actually break through the cordon to get at the girls to stop the fight. There were several incidents like that in the first year – fights between girls over boys which were set up by boys; they were in a sense 'promotional managers'. I'd never seen anything like it.

It was because of this that I asked very early after I'd been appointed what on earth we could do about it. We had to tackle sexism. That led to a discussion at a whole-school policy meeting which was an open forum for educational decisions, not administrative matters. It was an executive body. Decisions were made there and made democratically. I put sexism on the agenda. A lot of staff at that time thought this was a joke. And whilst there was a nucleus of support for looking at gender issues there was a lot of antagonism – not so much open opposition as cynicism, ridicule and so on, mainly from male members of staff. But the meeting set up a working party and that's still in place 12 years later.

I suppose in any school there are a few people who feel strongly about equal opportunities but don't feel that their views would be supported. They were keeping quiet if you like. And once the lid was taken off then they came out and said, 'Yes, we agree with you'. But more significantly I was very lucky in that I took over at a time when we were still expanding. So within two years we'd appointed almost 20 new teachers and four-fifths of the working party were new staff. So that's where the driving force came from.

Now I don't know whether they'd had working parties in the past but I think the feeling was, 'Well, I'll let a working party get on with it; it's not going to affect me'. And they couldn't, as it turns out, have been more wrong. But it was a way of marginalising it. I think that's how a lot of people saw it. And members of the working party came in for a good deal of stick one way or another. People didn't see it as the head's policy decision but as something somehow less serious – the head's got this bee in his bonnet and they've got a working party – so what? But within about three months, when the working party got very, very active and started doing things, then the balloon went up.

The working party was very aware of staff attitudes so it decided that if it was going to be successful it had to start by being pretty non-confrontational (although a lot of us felt confrontational, particularly the women members but they understood the reasons for not being so to start with). We felt we had to take fairly low-key issues to start with that would not be too controversial. We felt that we needed to go very slowly, a step at a time, and not try and take on the world over night. So we planned to identify an area or a target or an activity and tackle that and only when we'd tackled that successfully would we move on to something else.

So the first two or three meetings we spent listing things that we needed to give our attention to and deciding where we were going to start. And we decided collectively that we would start with the form names. Every form was named after a white male and a large proportion of them were famous because of their military exploits, so we had Nelson, Raleigh and Cromwell, for instance. We decided that we would change the form names and we would have a mixture of male and female, they would be multi-ethnic and they would be more in keeping with the school's identified philosophy. This was intended to be a small, uncontroversial first step.

Looking back I can laugh about it but at the time it was horrendous. I had two people come into this office and bang on my desk and said that they were going to resign. Some people called an emergency staff meeting without my knowledge. This was the end of the world, the pits! It was unbelievable! Unwittingly, the working party ended up going straight in! There were staff who didn't speak to some members of the working party for months as a result. We went ahead and, you know, it wasn't difficult going ahead in one sense in that I was able to say, 'Look. The whole-school policy meeting set up a working party and it had a brief and the brief was published and it was to identify sexism and then devise ways of combatting it, and what we are proposing is entirely within the brief. If you can put up cogent educational or other reasons why we shouldn't go ahead then we'll listen to you'. And so we went ahead. And that had two significant effects. The first was it had an effect on the working party because they realised that sexism was a hell of a lot more controversial than they thought. They had totally underestimated the strength of feeling. And the people who weren't on the working party realised we were serious. It wasn't a joke. And that, I would say, was the first major effect.

There was another one soon afterwards because the working party decided that their second task would be to ensure that all lists of pupils were done alphabetically. We thought this would be plain sailing after the last one! It was presented to meetings of the five pastoral teams, in their year groups, and it went on to all five agendas on the same evening and two of the tutors refused. One year tutor (who's long since left us) came back and told me it was illegal, it *had* to be boys and girls. I said, 'Well, you find me the legislation and I'll look at it myself!' All sorts of spurious reasons were put forward to prevent it from happening. And when the year group lists were being typed in the summer holidays in the school office in preparation for September, despite the fact that I had made it clear what we were going to do, two year tutors had not made any changes – they'd had the lists typed as boys and girls. They were typed by a woman who was basically opposed to what we were doing and was siding with the male year tutors. None of them are here now. But that was what it was like.

I think the best decision we made was to take one thing at a time: don't try and do too much at once because there's a tremendous danger that nothing works and then people can say, 'Well I told you it wouldn't work; I told you it was a flash in the pan' and so you don't make any progress. It seems silly to talk about an order of priorities – how can you say that putting names in alphabetical order is less or more important than the analysis of teaching material or looking at examination results? They're *all* important. It's very difficult to prioritise. And it may well be that the best way forward is to decide what you're going to do based on a likely success rate. Choose something that's going to be successful and that has a fairly quick return – that isn't going to take you three years to achieve – so that people can feel you're making progress. I think that's been a hallmark of the working party's work. They felt they were always making progress because they kept turning their attention to something and working on it and succeeding with it and then moving on to something else. It developed a momentum. And we've used that model in other working parties. The other thing is that there's never been any complacency. There still isn't. My advice would be, 'You've never finished! Never believe you've done it, because you haven't.'

I've been a member of the working party all the time. That's not because I felt I had an obligation as head teacher. I've done it out of personal interest and commitment. It's something which I feel very strongly about and it's something that I would never give up.

The membership of the working party changed, of course, and it has always been voluntary, like all our working parties, and we were never short of members. People have sometimes stepped down because they felt they'd done their whack or because they'd taken on new responsibilities in school and something had to go. New staff have joined it. We have more men on now than we did in the early days – four active men on the working party. At the last meeting a couple of weeks ago one of the things we were discussing was the male/female balance on the staff: it is much closer to 50: 50 than the 80: 20 we started with, but there still aren't a sufficient number of good male role models in terms of attitudes to gender and we were discussing how we can work more on male colleagues' attitudes.

If you look at fourth year option choices, we were starting from a position where only girls did textiles, only boys did design and technology (it was craft in those days). Hardly any boys did home economics, very few boys did modern languages, and this was heavily reinforced by parents: you'd be talking to a parent at parents' evening, saying, 'I think Sylvia really ought to consider design and technology' and the reply would be 'Oh, she doesn't want to do that; she needs to do cooking' and so on. That has changed considerably.

Parents have started to change their views as a result of reading school publications, the school newsletter, or some of the information sheets intended for students. There's been a consistent approach with students over time which I think has an effect at home. A lot of kids will go home and say what they've done. For example, the residential gender courses that we ran – originally we ran them for a week and now we've cut them to two or three days – but kids will go home and say, 'We've spent the last three days discussing gender' or, 'Next week I'm going to be on a gender course'. And I think a lot of the education of parents has been done by kids. We've educated the kids and the kids have educated their parents. They have challenged parental attitudes as a result of us raising their awareness about gender issues. It's happened in all sorts of ways: students going out on work experience in the fifth year, for example, where we looked at the patterns compared to ten years ago. And boys will now look at opportunities as secretaries in offices and girls will come and look at opportunities for work in an engineering workshop – and we'll argue that with their parents when it's necessary. So I think most of the effect on parents has been indirect, not direct.

I think it's probably fair to say that the reason we haven't done anything more directly with parents is lack of time and resources. This is always a problem for schools. We decided that our first and foremost responsibility is to the kids and second to the parents. We've had parents' evenings, we've had displays of gender material. We've had a theatre production: we brought in a feminist theatre group which some parents came to – not very many, but they don't come to many theatre productions full stop, never mind gender theatre productions. We had a women's week. We also had a women's festival five or six years ago and parents were invited into a lot of things that were going on. But that's been tinkering in a way – the main thrust of our work has been with kids and not with parents.

We've also developed a very strong policy on violence, physical and verbal, and we have very few fights here now. We will not tolerate that, and any student who physically attacks any other student is automatically excluded. It may be for a day, or more. We automatically see the parents and it goes all the way down the line. It doesn't matter who they are, what the circumstances, we will not tolerate it. And gradually that's brought about a significant change in behavioural patterns.

There are two strategies in place at the moment. One is to go on looking. The working party has a watching brief, if you like. It's looking for examples of sexism and as soon as it spots them it does something about them. Recent examples? Well, we felt very strongly about 12 months ago about the level of sexual harassment of some of the girls by boys and we've done a lot of work as a result and that's still going on. But in addition to that there are things that we identified a long time ago that you can go on working at forever, you never stop. The area where we have so far been least successful is the classroom itself – in terms of use of language by teachers, language by students and the notice teachers give or don't give to the language children use. They don't often enough correct language which is sexist or sexist attitudes in the classroom and they often use sexist language themselves. Not only language but modes and styles of learning, boys' dominance of space, boys' dominance of teachers, and so on. There are many classroom issues which we're working at.

At the last working party meeting we decided to devote the next meeting exclusively to one issue – sexist language. We are quietly collecting examples of sexist language around the school and we're writing them down whenever we hear them, anonymously. And we're going to create large cards with actual examples on them and we're going to come in at the weekend and going to plaster the staffroom walls with them and have a banner saying, 'Do you tolerate sexist language in your classroom?' It will be a surprise. Staff will be told that these have all been overheard in the last three months in the school, said either by students or by staff, and we'll ask them to listen out for more and to fill in some of the extra blank cards that we'll put in the staffroom during the week. We're going to have a week on it in an attempt to raise awareness in a very forcible but entertaining way so that people can go in and say, 'My God! That was me!' Ten years ago we would probably have had a riot but now members of staff will take it in good part and enter into the spirit of it and I think it will be a very positive week.

Emma's story

When I came here, the school was quite sexist in lots of ways. I observed that if a man was late for a lesson, a senior colleague would have a quiet word, but I actually saw women who had been late being man-handled. And I remember a male colleague saying to me soon after I arrived – I was appointed as 'pastoral' deputy – 'Why are you bothering with that girl? She is a slag and all her sisters have been the same. There is no point in talking to her.' Then there was the way that classrooms were set out, boys and girls in rows. And assembly! I couldn't believe my first assembly. I am sitting up on the stage with the management team and the boys were at one side with male teachers and the girls the other. That was about four years ago.

Two things helped get things moving. One was a document that came from the LEA (Local Education Authority) on equal opportunities policies for schools. The other was the school's being a TVEI pilot school and of course equal opportunities was supposed to underpin everything that took place.

So I organised this group by inviting people to join me and people did come forward. There was a great response from women on the staff who felt that changes needed to happen. I'd wanted a representative from each curriculum area but most of the people that came forward were (a) women and (b) low status. So I got this group together and at that time I didn't really know what we were going to do.

I started with a group because that was the practice that I was used to at my last school and I also felt that for some years my new school had been very much about one person making decisions and clearly staff wanted consultation and I felt that that was the best way forward.

One of the things that the members of the group had to do was to go back to their departments and disseminate what we had been doing so that things would trickle through at that level. Our brief was to feed back to the LEA within a year, through our governing body, what we were doing about equal opportunities. We met fortnightly for two terms after school in our own time. There were about ten of us.

In advance of starting these meetings I gathered together as much material as I could. I'd been going to conferences for years and knew a number of people nationally. I wrote to many of the ILEA teachers' centres for materials and I looked at the Gender Watch stuff. Although I had a reasonable awareness myself, through personal experience and through the work in my last school, a number of colleagues in the group were very worried. They wanted to be in on this, they felt it was a burning issue, but they didn't know how to cope with it and where to begin. So we watched videos, we looked at materials, we did some observation training in classrooms. We looked at assemblies and we looked at our registers. That was one of the first things we did, we altered the registers. A simple thing like that and yet it caused mayhem for some staff. When I went to check the registers, having talked to staff about it and agreed a policy, I found that two male members of staff – both heads of department – had underlined the boys' names in red. The reason for this they said was quite often the girls are down at PE or swimming and it is easier to pick out the boys' names than having to read through and find them! I had to ask them to re-write the register. This involved a good hour's conversation about what the school was doing, and the things they had always done and were comfortable with. In the end I said we could have longer conversations about these issues but I'm asking you now to re-write the register.

The group had open meetings and the new head was very, very supportive and came to them. We circulated all staff with minutes so that every member, including non-teaching staff and the caretaking staff, got minutes; nobody could see us as an exclusive group. We invited people to drop in on our meetings and to stay if they wished. People didn't come to begin with, and then as minutes trickled through, some people did. I remember once we had a black careers officer come. We were looking at gender and race. We didn't look at class at that time or disability because we felt we could only cope with two things and these were the prominent problems in this school. He talked to us about what it felt like to be black in this country, to be educated in an all-white school, to be the only black boy in the A stream and then to go on to university.

Over the two terms we met we were actually feeling quite good about what we were doing as a group and the trickling through of the ideas. Some people were coming back and saying, 'God. I had a terrible meeting with my department' and we were able to support one another with strategies on how to cope.

We weren't making any decisions at this time. It was merely a pulling together of research and our ideas for the school and we fed things back through the normal departmental or staff meetings. In public settings people did not make open derisory comments, but there was a certain attempt to trivialise the work: 'Why are we bothering? There are more important things to do'. But interestingly, because we were a TVEI pilot school and doing a lot of work on new teaching methods, that was making it more possible to look at what was going on in classrooms and to begin to change. The LEA was also organising meetings at the time so we actually met, three or four of us from a few schools, and started a cross-school support group. We met in pubs and we looked at what each school had been trying to do and the things we could share and try out.

The next thing was talking at the governors' meeting about our work. We've always had really good governors, very aware people and one of them had worked in the race relations area. I prepared a paper and said this is what we plan to do for awareness raising and one of them said, 'Yes, but what have you done? How is the school *changing*?' That response had a positive impact on us.

And then there's a thing about ability. This is a mixed-ability school and in each class you have got a few who are very able. The fashionable thing is not to work terribly hard but to have fun. So the girls are in a difficult situation because girls do tend to work harder and if they're bright they're getting stick not only from boys but from other girls too. So we felt that was something we needed to concern ourselves with and we started what became a regular opportunity for assertiveness training for girls.

We also decided that we needed to come up with an equal opportunities policy for school which was based on the problems that teachers were experiencing. So we identified the problems and suggested a number of possible strategies. The problems were to do with sexist remarks, racist remarks, racist graffiti, sexist graffiti, remarks in the yard, in the dinner queue, anywhere. Non-teaching staff were involved as well as teaching staff and we took the outcome to the governors and to the staff and we also had workshops for parents. There was also by this time a pupil working group chaired by the head of humanities. The pupils asked for a group because they were aware of what was happening from their lessons in guidance. They were mainly girls that came forward. And they started by doing some research on materials in humanities, the images that came across from the books, and discussed how you could confront these images and make them more positive. They presented their findings to a staff meeting and as a result a couple of other departments said they would be happy for the pupil group to work with them because they wanted to review resources as well. This was something that was manageable for pupils to do, something that could get them working cooperatively with staff, and something that wasn't going to confront staff too dreadfully. The pupils also helped with the policy document. They were the ones that gave us information as to what it was like and what happened in the yard. And things were much worse than we had thought. Staff awareness only skims the surface.

Then we decided to have a workshop for staff. I think that was the most difficult time I've ever had in a school. Staff realised that we were serious and that it was going to affect their classroom and they became quite worried and backtracked a lot. Clearly equal opportunities does affect your own value system and if you take it seriously it makes you question a lot of things – your upbringing, the way you behave to other people . . . What we were saying was that we've all talked about these things, we're all aware but we've now got a code of conduct and we expect you as members of staff to support it. Racist or sexist comments were not to be tolerated and any pupil using them would be excluded.

This clearly was likely to cause some difficulties. I remember being surprised by a particular incident involving a male head of department who was taking a group of fifth year boys down to Wimbledon. They sat in the back row of the coach and part way down the coach stopped so that people could have a snack. The boys started chatting to a group of mainly Asian girls from another school and their bus followed ours down the motorway. These lads, unknown to any of the teachers, wrote posters and bunged them onto the back seats so that the girls could see. It was only when they got to Wimbledon that the staff realised that they were awful – sexist and racist. The head of department, despite the fact that he's a tennis fan, said they were not going into Wimbledon and neither would he. He sat them in various points on the bus for four hours while everybody else watched the match and he refused to let them speak to one another. The next day at school he showed me the evidence and we excluded them. Photocopies were sent home to their parents and they were not allowed to return to school for two days. All the parents but one were supportive. One said: 'I am racist. I support the National Front. And if my son is, then that's fine by me'. I said:

'Well it's not fine by me and if you cannot support the school in what we're trying to do then I suggest that your son goes to another school'. He backed off then and compromised: 'I don't agree with you but if he is in this school then I'll make sure that I support you in that respect'.

The policy also affected staffroom behaviour and that caused some problems to begin with – a bit of trivialisation and I remember not knowing how to cope with it to begin with. I used to go into the staffroom and people would say, 'Oh, hang on. Can't say that. Emma's here'. Eventually I learned not to respond, just to smile sweetly and in time it stopped.

So we piloted the policy for a term and during that term we had some workshops for parents. Most of these went quite well but there were some difficult parents. I showed one group a video of women in non-stereotypical jobs and there was a parent whose daughter was in our fifth year, and he had just been made redundant and he made a personal response to the video: 'That is why there are so many people unemployed. It's all these bloody women back at work'. And he came up to me afterwards and said, 'And I suppose you've got kids have you? Well, you should be at home looking after them instead of out at this time of night'. He became confrontational and as he left he ripped three of the equal opportunities posters off the wall and binned them. There were other problems, slightly less confrontational, like a mother saying she'd had two daughters go through this school, both of whom had gone on to college and that 'they never needed all this claptrap about sexism'.

We tried a bit of work with our feeder schools so that they knew what we were about and we also, almost inadvertently, got the local FE (Further Education) college involved. I'd taken a group up, a fifth year guidance group, and when we got there some staff took us round in smaller groups. One of the staff said, at one point: 'I'll just take the lads now and show them the engineering department because the girls won't be interested'. I didn't say anything but one of the girls said, 'Well, actually we are interested. I want to do science A levels and I wanted to go on to do engineering. And we've had the WISE [Women Into Science and Engineering] bus in'. Instead of realising he'd put his foot in it he went on and said, 'I've yet to meet a decent female engineer'. Well the pupils quite frankly took him apart. I didn't have to say a thing. They complained officially before we left. The very next day another group went and had a similar experience and the senior member of staff responsible for relations with schools rang up and said, 'What the bloody hell are you doing? I've now got staff who refuse to show your pupils round'. And I said this is a serious problem. You've got to move your college along. Since then I've actually run a couple of workshops there.

It's never been easy. Even small things. Our indoor corridors are terribly dull so I had the pupils do ten large murals on the theme of equal opportunities and the theme was carried through into all classrooms and corridors.

Staff tried to dismiss it by saying the school looked like a nursery school, but I took that as a compliment!

We also tried to work on our governors. For a while we had a thing called 'governor of the month' where we invited a governor each month to come in and look particularly at the equal opportunities work and talk to the pupils. At this time we also made sure that all pupils in the school encountered equal opportunities formally within the curriculum through their guidance and PSE [Personal and Social Education] work; the concerns were also reflected in other areas of the curriculum.

After a term of piloting and working on outside links, it was agreed that the policy should be accepted and it went into the staff handbook and into the parents' handbook. Interestingly, from then on, for the next 18 months, it was tempting to think we'd got there. But if at that time you breathe a sigh of relief it could just disappear from under your noses. So periodically there have been injections of activity. For instance at the moment there's worry about our fourth year pupils under-performing and those worries are related to gender issues. We're also concerned to see what's actually happening in classrooms. There's no longer a need for a formal working party – but staff continue to meet informally. We also tried to extend the work to race because there was a tendency for staff to feel because we have very few black pupils that 'there is no problem here'.

I think what we have done so far is change behaviour but we haven't altered attitudes, I don't think, and it is attitudes that count. And I believe that the only way we'll do that is by working with children from nursery education right through so that they get the same messages. Within the school I want to see our heads of department being much more proactive in all manner of ways with gender and equal opportunities. I want them to take more responsibility for what's actually happening in the department and in people's classrooms. A particular problem is that this area produces girls who are bright but still will not go for what they're capable of. They under-sell themselves at careers interviews – loads of them are like that.

Looking back, the highs have been the kids' growing awareness, because they *will* change things. If we actually get this generation to believe that this is important then they're going to effect change. Also there's the change in some of the staff. There are a few staff here who in the beginning I thought were almost no-hopers in terms of equal opportunities and they've gone through quite a painful process and they're now supportive and aware, not just supportive in a passive way.

The lows have quite often been to do with difficult staff who say, 'I don't believe in this' and you see that these people are not prepared to move at all. There are two or three still with us after four years of work. We've also had some difficult times with some parents. It has been a struggle and it continues to be a struggle but I think it's been the most fascinating and intense thing I've ever done.

Fran's story

I suspect that one of the things that determined how I acted here is how it was in my last school. That was a school that was in many ways conservative with a small 'c'. I'm talking about the late 1970s, early 1980s. But there had been a group of women, I think they were all women, perhaps there was one bloke involved, who had tried to talk about gender issues. It was a very large staff and one of the things that happened, and I'm not sure why, was it alienated the staff. The management were resistant to it because they were suspicious of it and didn't understand it. And there was also that inverted thing where other women say, 'Look. There isn't a problem'. It was dreadful to watch it – at that time I had my own failure of nerve because I wasn't involved in that group. The people who started it didn't do it in a particularly open way but ultimately they made a presentation, which was actually very good, but the group was completely marginalised and nothing happened except it allowed all sorts of prejudices to come out. The group were all fairly junior and it was unfair [that they were rejected] because they had things to say. Some of the group left and some stayed but the cohesion didn't exist any more; they didn't have an input to the public debate.

I was aware that I shared many of their views but I had that hesitancy – and I'm not very proud of it – because I thought it wouldn't do me much good to be personally associated with what they were doing. When you're more secure about your own professional position you can afford to do that. In fact, a lot of the women in the school did feel alienated, did feel that they weren't valued, but their way of earning status was to make themselves indispensable in traditional ways, to play this subservient role. It used to annoy me. And there were people who were much more open than me and said, 'I'm not doing that. You're expecting me to do it because I'm a woman'. And they were much more challenging. Also I used to hate the derogatory remarks about 'pushy women' which was a way of putting down those who spoke out.

I am interested in the confrontations that happen in schools, disagreements between staff – you see them in every staff room – and most are to do with values and attitudes. I knew we could all agree what colour we're going to paint this, that and the other but if you want to make decisions about some of the bigger issues you need an awareness of why we all take the stance we do. My theory was that when things fall apart it's because people of very different values have united behind the same idea but they've united behind it often for very different reasons; [the differences haven't been explored and] there comes a point at which it pulls apart. People have to be prepared to explore things at a personal level.

When I came to my present school I came as one of two new deputy heads and equal opportunities was in the job descriptions. This school was actually saying it valued it because it was in both deputy head job descriptions. And there was a decision that we'd work on equal opps together. I have a view of equal opps that encompasses special needs and the other deputy (a man) had a wealth of experience on racial issues that I didn't have and so it became a double act.

I personally didn't like the way that we might be seen as 'the new regime'. But we asked if we could do a school review. The hidden reason for doing that was to say to the staff: 'You've been here a lot longer than us and we recognise that and we're asking you what you think this school should be doing.' Equal opps was mentioned by some staff along with a lot of other things. We were then able to feed the list back and to highlight (a) those that they felt were whole-school issues and (b) those that they thought might be for working parties. Equal opps ended up being in both areas: they said it ought to be a working party *and* a whole-school issue. Now there were two very different reasons for saying it should be a working party. There were the teachers who were the vanguard, who felt we have something to say quite strongly and we want a forum where we can say it. And there were others who thought, I'm not interested, it's not a whole-school issue, a little group can do it if they want to. A much larger number of people recognised it was a big issue and that if it was to be addressed it had to involve everybody in the school.

When you're new you don't pick all the different vibes up, but I was gradually beginning to find out how people saw equal opps. Something had been attempted in the past: quite a while ago a female deputy had done registers and assemblies and that sort of thing, so a lot of the things that are obvious starters had been done and had been quite well received. But then there'd also been a group that had met; people felt that these colleagues had got points to make that were tied up with their political and social values – which inextricably they are. I was aware of being given a lot of versions of history, and I picked up negative ones about the equal opps work. It just made me cautious and what I decided was that the first thing was you can't afford to be dismissed by fulfilling all the stereotypes. So I was quite convinced we were not going to have a group of 'junior women' with a benevolent female deputy. I thought, 'We will have people of some status, we will have men, we will have people who might traditionally not be seen to have had sympathy for equal opps'. And I did a lot of ground work, and I invited these people into the group. And so we had a working group that met during the final term of last year. I wrote the brief trying to bear in mind what people had said during the review, what we felt as management, and what I felt I'd picked up from the staff. One of the aims was just to prepare a group of people who would be able to lead the school through a public debate and to do some clarifying of our own views.

We had a good group. We went through issues for us, issues for the school, and then we did a bit of exploratory work, and at the end we did some prioritising. And it was also important that both the deputies were in that group; I've always felt it's important that it's not just the female deputy. We also did some work on other aspects of denied opportunity. We then set ourselves up for a biggie – a public statement: the second staff meeting of the year was to be devoted to equal opps. That was the beginning of my second year. And again I tried to think really hard about how we presented it. In the end I worked with a junior colleague; she was the TVEI equal opps representative and she had a real interest in the work. So she and I planned the evening, although I introduced it and I tried deliberately to say that there are legislative reasons why equal opps is on the map and there are our own feelings, but also there are valid educational reasons. That was my major point: there are valid educational reasons for addressing this issue. Saying this can stop those people who might want to marginalise it. People can easily say it's just a group of women promoting themselves, being assertive – they actually mean being aggressive – but I'm not into allowing people to marginalise equal opps issues in that way. So I was all for the public management statement offering valid educational reasons.

We'd briefed the group leaders, who were all working party members. We were all agreed that we weren't about alienating staff, but we were about getting some issues out into the open. And if you have a list of things which people have to prioritise you don't really allow them to disagree with them. I mean it's a way of being very positive about getting into something. People said to us quite directly at the end of that staff meeting, 'Yes, actually we think quite a lot of these things are important but we need some suggestions please about how to start'.

So we got together an information pack and we tried to put in lots of practical stuff about checking for classroom behaviour, some really good key questions, and we used some of the Gender Watch stuff. We did four packs and we put people into four curriculum faculties in order to look at them. Now there was a reason for putting them in faculties. This school is small. We have departments of ones and twos, and if you're getting to grips with an issue you've got nothing to bounce off. And if you just keep certain people with well entrenched views together, you're never going to stimulate the sort of debate, friendly or otherwise, which just might make people reconsider. So there were other reasons why I wanted to establish 'faculty' groupings to discuss things which were not the traditional departmental ones. We put maths and science together, we put together a communications faculty, a creative faculty, and a humanities faculty.

Each had a pack of resources but in fact it floundered. I expected people to do something: because they had led me to believe that they wanted to do it, I expected that they would. Some did, but it was very hit and miss. I hadn't judged correctly the varying degrees of confidence among colleagues. We had some inservice money left and as the inservice coordinator it was easy for me to say, 'If you want some time to consider how to use these materials you can have some money'.

It was in fact a 'twilight' training session for all staff, linked to TVEI, that provided the opportunity to follow up on the curriculum angle – we judged that many people would feel safest with that. We asked colleagues to decide what it was that they were going to look at from a curriculum point of view and to actually begin some planning there and then, and to give minutes to us. People sat down and wrote things. We hadn't got empty words. It struck me as being genuine. We've had, since then, people say, 'Right. We've done a lot of work. Now you (meaning us – management) how do you know that it's actually hitting the classrooms?' And of course that is the crucial question. So I'm going round to a lot of colleagues talking to them and I'm picking up messages about changes in actual classrooms, and we've set one or two items for future professional development days which are building on things that people have said they want to do. We've got groups working on links with parents and others on the school environment. And we've decided that one of our professional development days is going to be on display – presentation of images – in the public arena.

That's the stage that we're at. Staff are thinking and they are asking management to help them do things. Some teachers here were doing things on equal opps long before I came and they're still doing that work. It's just that equal opps didn't have a platform. I think the other thing is that there are members of staff who know that making something your own by giving utterance to it is an important part of the learning. There's a lot of oral work here, group work, and the kids are therefore confident and able to discuss things. Equal opps benefits from that kind of teaching style.

Some of our pupils are from the Church School and that gives us some middle class kids. But our other feeder schools draw from the estate. This would be a social priority school simply because of the influx – some families are being deliberately moved into the estate, problem families that have been brought in or single parent families. There's a lot of bigotry and prejudice. You're aware of the racism. Now it may be that on the surface this school seems not to have problems. We don't have many black kids so we don't see fights that are about colour. But that's too simplistic. Racism is a problem in this school and that is also something that the staff want to tackle.

I'm aware that so far I've not really involved parents – because I'm aware of all their prejudices. If I'm busy dealing with a group of staff I don't really want to take on the parents as well. When I do talk to the parents I want to be sure how I'm going to do it because you can't afford to mess that one up. I've seen it elsewhere: they say, 'Right. We're going to talk to parents about this' and they've alienated them. I'm not for tackling that one head on until I'm secure. We've resurrected the Parents Association. And we've got an excellent governing body. And if you just build up all sorts of mutual regard then I'll be ready to chance talking with parents about issues of equal opps. I suppose I'm being cautious, but I think rightly so.

GENERAL REFERENCE

Kate's story

What happened at my last school

I'd been on some inservice training, was very very enthusiastic and I asked the head for permission to set up an equal opportunities working party. He gave that permission. I made it open to anybody on the staff and nine people joined – only two of the nine were men. One was a deputy head who said, 'I've been sent along to keep an eye on things', and one was the TVEI coordinator who said, 'I'm here because equal opps is one of the TVEI priorities'. They weren't committed but they joined and eventually both of them played a really full part. I invited outside speakers and the enthusiasm to push forward was even greater.

After eight months we approached the head and said we would like time out of school to write a gender policy, which we did, and we found it very easy; we were all in agreement, we all knew what needed to be done. We wrote a very long, very detailed policy.

At that point we asked for inset for the staff and we were given permission straight away to have a whole day. And the day was an absolute disaster. We tried to cover equal opps in all its forms – gender, race and disability – with outside speakers, with workshops. The depth of prejudice, lack of knowledge, the fears that people had about equal opps were in many cases very deep seated and we'd gone in far too quickly and far too profoundly. Some people were with us straight away, some were sceptical but willing to give things a try, but quite a number of people – and people who were in key posts – were absolutely devastated. They either felt guilty or antagonistic and we found ourselves quite unable to cope with a lot of the things that came back to us. We found it very difficult to help people over the hurdles that really we'd created.

I left the school at that point and the group carried on with the work but in a much more low key way. Something that stayed with me was the idea that if you start a working party up you get the committed, while other individuals need time to work through slowly and carefully with you what you're wanting to change and how you're wanting to change it.

Moving to the Avenue School

I was appointed as TVEI coordinator. When I first came I explained to colleagues how the Authority's TVEI submission was about enhancing the *entire* secondary curriculum, that priorities were set out, and that only if we pushed those priorities forward would we keep getting the money. TVEI has several priorities of which equal opps is one.

I looked at the priorities with the head and we talked about where he would feel happiest with me making a start. He wanted me to make IT across the curriculum the main thrust. I mentioned equal opps and said it was a particular interest of mine and I would like to at least *start* doing some work. The response was really, 'All right, but talk to the senior staff about everything you want to do and don't go off at a tangent'. So although there was a commitment to pursuing it, as there was with all the TVEI priorities, it hadn't been identified as a priority for this school by the senior management.

Now this is a school where very few of the senior staff are female – just two out of 13. The school staff were well aware that of the first 16 TVEI appointments in the Authority, 14 were white strapping males; TVEI had got quite a masculine image. It was only in the second round of appointments, when I was appointed, that more women began to join the team. So the school expected a man for TVEI. Also they didn't have many role models of women being involved in technology. And they didn't have any role models of females at middle management level. So in many ways I had to show them that I could do the job, that I could do it well and in this way build up a sense of trust in my own competence.

There was a period when people just waited to see what happened. They weren't antagonistic but they weren't necessarily in favour. I had to prove myself and that is why I left equal opps alone at first to get some kind of credibility on the other things. I put a lot of effort into IT across the curriculum – that improved everybody's picture of what TVEI offered. I tried to make it very supportive. It was people identifying their own needs, a lot of classroom-based inset, working with members of staff and with groups of pupils in the actual classroom for long periods of time. And so, over 12 months, people gradually got to use computers in every area of the school bar one, where the resistance remained. Again, within technology, people came to me with something they wanted to do and if it fitted, even vaguely, under the TVEI umbrella I would find them people to talk with in the city, and would pay for resources. So they very quickly saw me as a source of support, human and financial. Yes there was distrust in the beginning but that quickly dissipated.

But I didn't let the year go by and just neglect equal opps. To start with it was very much a softly, softly approach. I tried to raise it at senior management level in a gentle way, to raise it with committees and to work with individuals and with small groups and build it up gradually.

What I did was I selected various people and put suggestions to them about small events, small changes. So rather than saying anything to the staff as a whole I selected individuals, often because I had felt there was resistance there, and worked with them slowly and carefully. For example, I talked to a newly appointed IT coordinator who didn't really think that girls-only groups had much to offer. I gave him the chance to talk to the girls them-selves, to talk to other members of staff, and then one female colleague suggested setting up a girls-only computer club. He didn't really feel threatened by then – he thought there was a good reason for it, understood that it wasn't discriminating against boys. Only a few girls joined but she took that group forward.

And I talked at length to one of the heads of year about the fourth year girls (year 10) and about the small number that were involved in electronics or business studies courses where they use machinery. We talked to girls, talked to other members of staff and then we arranged a four-day programme, girls only, to work on electronics to boost their confidence and improve their skills. We gave them evaluation sheets and they were fascinating reading because a lot of them said how different it was to work away from boys who constantly elbowed them out of the way of computers, who told them they couldn't do any soldering. I made sure the evaluation sheets were seen by a lot of people – I just offered them as something they might like to think about. That helped one or two people who are in traditional male areas to get some insight into what girls' only groups can do.

Then I suggested that we book the WISE bus for the year 9 girls. By the time I made this suggestion people who had been fairly anti were beginning to see the reasons for it and I persuaded two female members of staff to actually take an assembly for the girls, explaining why we were having it and what we hoped they might gain from it. There was quite a lot of support by then for this kind of thing.

This was going on last year – small groups, only a few members of staff each time, plenty of time for discussion – just picking off little bits and pieces and making sure they got a lot of publicity round the school. When little openings presented themselves I grasped them – so, yes, a mixture of a plan of campaign and opportunity.

And I tried to help the image of equal opps along. For example, I alerted the local paper to the WISE bus and we got pictures in the paper, lots of comments from the girls about how exciting it was. People in school feel that anything that gives good publicity is great.

I always made it clear that if people had any real reservations, then, fine, we wouldn't do it yet, we'd wait a while. I think I paid attention to creating an aura of safety and support. I made sure that anything that's useful to read is around – non-threatening materials, full of positive suggestions – and I didn't necessarily chase it up or ask people whether they'd read it and what they were feeling about it.

I wanted a whole-school inset session but that proved extremely difficult to organise. Equal opps wasn't high up on the senior management team's [SMT] list of priorities. We did set a date but I was told records of achievement were much more pressing. Three more dates were set and each time other things moved up the list of priorities. I think SMT were genuine in saying other things were more important. They didn't see equal opps as a problem. It's helping them to see it as a problem that's the difficulty. The people who create the agenda are men and it's difficult for a woman's voice to be heard, particularly at senior management level. I wasn't part of any of the senior management groups and there wasn't really much in the way of female representation.

Almost two years after I was appointed we got a commitment to having an inset half-day on equal opps where people could stand back, look at the issues, look at the evidence, look at statistics and look at what a whole-school approach to equal opps might actually mean. I invited a woman called Isabel Shepherdson, an ex-head who has retired but puts all her efforts into equal opps gender work now. She's incredibly witty, she's incredibly humble, she talks about her career in teaching, the mistakes she made in trying to promote equal opps, the successes she had, the ways forward people can take. There was none of the accusation stuff: 'You've been holding the girls back'. I found that after that there was a real solid base to start from. It was very, very positive and so from then I've been able to move forward, I think, quite quickly.

A number of people approached me and said how for the first time they'd really appreciated what it was that equal opps was trying to achieve and how many things we were involved in which could be quite damaging to the girls and their self-esteem and that didn't actually help the boys either. They offered all sorts of useful and interesting ideas.

So during the summer I thought long and hard about what we might achieve, and I was fortunate in that the Authority was making some funding available for International Women's Day. Money is always a carrot to lure people with so I took advantage of the opportunity and sent all departmental heads a letter saying if there was anything they would like to pursue I would try to arrange funding for it. People were in favour but didn't quite know what sort of thing might be helpful so I went round with suggestions. We're getting a theatre in education company who will run a programme on gender stereotyping. The head of English agreed to build this into work with the year 9s. There'll be materials to work on in lessons, a workshop for the whole year and the final part will be a performance, which is evidently quite powerful and moving. And then a member of staff came to me and said that he knew a black woman writer and would like funding for her to come in and run a workshop with sixth form pupils, looking at gender. So we included that in our funding application.

So there's been a slow adoption of the principles of equal opps. And it hasn't only been the women – we have quite a lot of younger men who are supporters. It does tend to be the younger ones but some of the senior ones are becoming increasingly involved.

The only area that is very, very difficult to deal with is staffing and the allocation of allowances. I've tried to raise it and I've found that people at the top are resistant to looking at how the situation has arisen or what could be done. It seems that a lot of the women don't see themselves as being in a career. They have a job and they don't think there's a lot of possibility. They look round and they see their head of department, the head of year, their senior management team, virtually all male. If that attitude hardens in female members of staff, I think it must have an effect on the way female pupils think about themselves. I think the support is there now to change things for pupils but there is a resistance to accepting that role models have an impact and must be looked at if we're really going to change things. I'm well aware that if I make great waves and create antagonism it will undermine what I'm doing successfully here and in other areas. And yet I do feel in a sense that I'm selling people short because I'm not pushing it.

And then an encouraging thing happened: after I'd talked to the head about what I'd been doing in the school I was invited to join a senior planning group – which had been all-male. So, yes, I am making small inroads into some of the structures but I don't feel I'm doing much to generate discussion of why we have such a very male dominated hierarchy. Another encouraging thing was that I said to the head it might be time to change the titles from 'headmaster' and 'deputy headmaster' and 'deputy headmistress' and actually have non-sexist titles. I was trying to explain that equal opps wasn't only about doing positive things for girls with technology but that there was a whole complex background that gave girls limited ideas of what was possible for them. And he said it was fine so long as I paid for the new signs. So I took the old ones down, screwed the new ones back up and felt encouraged that the terminology was also changed in the letterheads. When people in the staff room became aware of what had happened it was all the usual banter but it was generally regarded as a positive move. I then spoke to all the year heads and asked whether there was anything particularly useful in having all the lists divided into girls and boys – always the boys first. I checked with the examinations officer to see if any exam entries had to be given in that way. I checked with the person who was organising the changeover in the office to computers to see whether there were any problems. It emerged that nobody could see any really useful purpose being served by the lists and so I asked whether it was a good time to start thinking about organising the lists alphabetically for next September. The head agreed and a note went out saying this. There were very small pockets of resistance but I dealt with each one on an individual basis, explained the reasons and how cumulative the effect of all these small and seemingly trivial things could actually be. I explained what it was like if you spent your life going from lesson to lesson hearing a register read out which made it clear that the most important thing about you is your gender and that boys always come first.

So, the work with the pupils is proving quite effective and I'm hoping that in this climate of acceptability that things to do with staffing will also be accepted. I want people to think about equal opps as a natural part of the way they work. I don't want them to think, 'Oh. Equal opps. Done that. Got the T-shirt'. I want to get to a point where if people are ordering books or buying posters they think, 'Are women shown doing active things?'. If there's a science book, are the women hanging around making a cup of tea in the background or are they in there carrying out experiments? I want them to open the door and say, 'Have you got six kids who could move a couple of tables for me?' instead of saying, 'Can I have six strong boys?'. The areas I want to move into next are classroom interaction and I think I've seen little openings there where I can talk about research which shows over and over again how much time we spend answering boys' questions leaving the quiet girls just to work away in the background. And I also want to work with the head of careers on work experience placements to see if we can do something about the stereotyping that goes on there.

Shortly after this interview was recorded, the LEA announced the reorganisation of secondary schools and heads were invited to submit a list of the posts they wanted in the future. In Kate's school it was decided that the responsibility for TVEI coordination was to be taken over by the senior management team. A new post in humanities was created which included responsibility for equal opps. Kate was urged to apply. She was not happy with equal opps being relocated outside TVEI and outside the traditional 'male' areas of IT, technology and industry links; she thought that such a move might lead to its marginalisation. At the same time she thought that if responsibility for TVEI coordination was taken on by named members of the senior management team, the head would be in a position to control and direct the resources that TVEI brought to the school and that this was very important at a time of rapid change.

She decided to apply for a post in another school. There had been 'plenty of praise for all my competence and organisational ability' but she wondered whether, within the new structure, equal opps would have a lower profile.

In fact, before she left, the head decided that there would not be a designated equal opps responsibility attached to any post in the school. However, by this time a number of staff had been supported in attending training sessions on gender run by the LEA. Enough committed and informed people were still at the school to enable Kate to feel that the work on equal opps would be kept alive.

Kate recognised how much she had done in building a climate in which work on gender could flourish, she recognised the importance of having resources to encourage people to take new things on, but she also acknowledged her own culpability in acting somewhat too independently of her senior management team, believing that they would endorse her actions on equal opps because she was successfully pursuing work on IT and technology that they had identified as their priorities for the school.

I do care about them (i.e. the senior management team) because they're colleagues and I try to look at it from their point of view and if you have been the chosen ones and you have been very powerful and everything has been as you wanted it to be, I do understand that it can be quite hard when people challenge the status quo and come up with what can seem quite alarming ideas about the kind of activities that we ought to engage in. If I was a white male having been in education for years and found it easy to get promotion and found myself surrounded by people that looked and acted just like me, change would feel quite threatening. So I retain an element of sympathy, but at the same time I do feel that they ought to be strong enough to face up to the staffing situation, to analyse it, and to move forward.

I've looked back at responses that often seemed supportive and realise that the feelings of threat were probably much stronger than I'd appreciated . . . Looking back, perhaps I didn't talk things through with senior management enough. I think I needed to spend more time keeping them informed . . . I think I've also learned that when people say, 'Yes, that's right. Go for it. We want that', that's not necessarily how they will feel when it happens.

Looking forward to the next post
As part of the reorganisation, every teacher in the Authority had to put three jobs down in order of preference. I put it as my first choice to go on doing the job I'd been doing at the Avenue School – but in another school.

The school I'm going to is an all-boys' school – ex-grammar and at the point of reorganisation it will be mixed. The staff is mostly male at the moment but it will have women in senior management. I chose to apply there because I see it as a real challenge to go into a school which they admit is very male oriented. It will have both boys and girls up to fourth year at the time of reorganisation, and a fourth, fifth and sixth form which is only boys. Within three years it will be totally mixed. I think to be in at the beginning and to have some kind of influence will be interesting and worthwhile. And I will be able to continue having input into all areas of the curriculum, which is important to me.

The final passage shows Kate reflecting on what she had learned from her work in the two schools:

As a result of these two experiences I'm building up an enormous filing system of ideas, strategies, things I've been surprised by, things I've been heartened by, and I think I'm able now to put together a package from all the tried-and-discarded and tried-and-adopted strategies from the past. Every experience is useful and often the most useful ones are the ones that are initially very hurtful. I think in future the warning bells will ring more loudly as I step into some situations . . . I don't think you ever do get it right – I just think you get slightly better at it. Somebody said to me that working in equal opps is like emptying the ocean with a teacup. When you're absolutely exhausted you stop doing it. I could feel that but on the other hand I say to myself, 'If we all keep going with our teacups then as long as we're strong enough in the end things will really change'.

Comment

Some common strands run across the four stories. First, there is the strength of the personal commitment of the gender leaders. This is important, for had it been less strong they might well have lost their nerve and transferred their attention to easier tasks. The strength of their commitment is related to their capacity to 'see through' some of the taken-for-granted features of school life. In each case they were helped, initially, by having, for a short but valuable time, the eyes of the stranger. While schools are similar in many respects and the sites and patterns of most acutely gendered practice are predictable, neverthe-less schools have different characters and cultures. Some of the gender leaders recalled a sense of shock as they observed certain features of their new schools: Geoff saw violence in the way that men related to women, boys related to girls, girls fought each other, in public contests, over boys. To a newcomer, the patriarchal structures were starkly exposed. Emma recalls the sharpness of the divisions – boys separated from girls in assembly and in registers; 'decent' girls separated in the structure of teachers' expectations from girls who lacked the comfortable com-pliance expected of females. And Kate saw the signs on senior col-leagues' doors as symbolising the male power that her work on gender set out to challenge. The sense of outrage released the energy to act. But, equally importantly, each of the gender leaders had, in their new roles, some formal authority that permitted them to act. Even Kate felt justified, as TVEI coordinator, in working on gender as well as tech-nology (which her head had directed her to) because she knew that it was one of the TVEI priorities; and she also knew that she could justify her action to others by explaining that continued TVEI funding was dependent on a school demonstrating that it was trying to move forward on *all* the TVEI priorities.

The stories that the gender leaders tell (although some of this may have been lost in the shortening) tend to be structured around critical incidents that carry a high emotional charge. For instance, there is Geoff's first encounter, as a new head, with a parent; there is Emma's confrontation with two male heads of department about changing the registers, or the time when, at the end of a gender evening for parents, a pupil's father ripped the gender posters down from the wall; there was the whole-staff event that went wrong for Kate, and Fran's realisation that the system she had worked so hard to set up was not being taken seriously by her colleagues. All these incidents, in one way or another, threatened the credibility and authority of the gender leaders – and this realisation, in the case of the women, was an additional layer of potential hurt.

There were also the critical periods which the gender leaders sensed at the time, or understood retrospectively, were turning points for the development of a whole-school policy. For Geoff, it was the occasion when staff realised that he really was serious, that this was not a 'bee in the bonnet' and that what he was trying to do had implications for them as individuals. At these make or break moments, if the gender leader is not a senior teacher in the school, the management team may – as happened in Kate's school – decide to rein in the work on equal opps. Or a new wave of minor hostility may break out. For the gender leaders, if this happens, the hope will be that the momentum for change is by now so strong that the members of the opposition will merely become marginalised moaners or be properly subject to some coercion on the part of senior management. And there may always be unexpected converts, like the male deputy in Kate's school who offered to represent the school on a local gender course, or Emma's male PE teacher who became aware, on an outing to Wimbledon, of the boys' harassment of some Asian girls from another school and instead of ignoring it or issuing a faint reprimand refused them entry and sat with them on the coach, missing all the play.

There are good moments, of course, but it takes courage to continue in the face of challenges and mockery – for instance, the pointed remarks that are made in the staff room when the gender leader comes in: 'You can't say that, Emma's here'. It also takes tremendous professionalism to maintain cordial relations – as head, or deputy, or TVEI coordinator – with colleagues whom you know are trying to trivialise the issues, or to block you. And it takes determination to continue when you realise how much effort has gone into getting things moving and how much there is still to be done in the school. And then there is the sense of frustration that comes from uncertainty about the longer term impact of work within the school if the structures and attitudes outside the school remain largely unchanged. Most gender leaders were uncertain whether they should attempt to work with parents and employers and, if so, how.

There are occasions when the gender leaders are faced by a serious dilemma. For instance, they may be pursuing a softly, softly approach in order to bring as many staff as possible with them when they realise that something has to be done about harassment in the school; they know that there is really no alternative but to tackle the problem urgently and fairly, for the discomfort caused by the enquiry will not be as great as the distress of those who have experienced abuse.

In short, taking initiatives that are controversial is not an easy responsibility. The gender leaders acknowledged periods of strain, doubt, anger and frustration. Their emotions were sometimes complicated and intensified by feelings of isolation. One teacher I interviewed, also a female deputy head, said that she had gone home and cried on several occasions because she did not know how to reconcile the wishes of her more radical colleagues, who wanted her to tackle gender in a more outspoken and confrontational way, with her own judgement that more would be effected in the school in the long run if she won colleagues over gradually. And another, in a different school, said that her worst moments were hearing colleagues, both female and male, ridicule her for setting up a support group for women teachers which was meeting on the school premises.

The gender leaders benefited from having people that they could talk things through with, either in the school or outside. They accepted that confrontation, at some level, was probably inevitable. They realised the importance of consultation and of keeping colleagues informed – both important factors in building up trust and a sense of whole-school responsibility. Overall, the pace of change was well judged and they managed to build up enough support, over time, to ensure that the work would not easily be undone even if they were to leave the school.

4 POINTS OF DEPARTURE

In the last chapter the ups and downs of working towards a whole-school gender policy were described from the perspective of the gender leaders themselves. The stories indicate the emotional strain, in some settings, of choosing to carry the banner openly, and the strategic and inter-personal skills needed to build support in settings where a direct appeal to principles of equality is risky. In this chapter the focus is more on strategies adopted: the starting points and the paths the initiatives took, in different settings, as they drew in more of the school's activities and staff.

In Castle School, the working party, which was set up at the suggestion of a new head who was committed to equal opportunities, used International Women's Day as an occasion for going public on gender, and built out confidently on a number of related pupil and parent-centred projects, taking advantage of opportunities for external support that presented themselves.

In St Benet's, the development is best characterised as 'supported natural growth'. Initially it was TVEI funding that legitimised collective action and a number of already interested departments got together and agreed to see what they could achieve in the space of a term. They demonstrated these achievements to the whole staff and the initiative started to spread through the curriculum. But this was in a school where an over-arching and clearly articulated concern for the welfare of pupils predisposed members of staff to look constructively at their daily practice in terms of gender – once the issue had been made visible.

In Forge School the appeal was also to a unifying principle but here it was 'professionalism'. The mark of the teacher as professional was interpreted as ensuring that no child is disadvantaged in relation to his or her right to achieve. An agenda was built up, logically, from this premise: the school focused on outcome statistics and on options patterns; it looked at – and worked on – attendance figures, destinations and local employment practices.

The accounts raise several issues that are worth reflecting on. One is the functioning of the gender, or equal opportunities, working groups which seem to be a feature of most approaches to gender, as the stories in the last chapter also indicated. Fran's story suggests that the title 'working group' can be interpreted by staff as a meeting that serves the interests of its members while a 'working party' is seen as acting on behalf of the whole staff. However, this distinction was not consistently maintained across the schools and the word 'group' was sometimes preferred because it had less of a bureaucratic ring to it.

A working group may be led by junior staff or by senior staff; it can invite volunteers, or members may be courted or detailed. It can seek coverage by requiring a representative from each department, it can go for opinion leaders on the staff, or it can try to recruit members of departments which traditionally have a gendered image. It can, of course, sometimes suit a head who is both ambivalent about equality issues and politically nervous to encourage interested but relatively junior teachers to set up a gender group in order to test the temperature; the head can then distance her or himself if the response is conflictual, or increase support and identification if reactions are more positive.

Volunteers can be effective if the school staff as a whole is reasonably harmonious in its support for gender, for then the group is likely to be – and to be seen to be – representative of the interests of the majority. If there is no such easy harmony, then the group (whether volunteers or selected) may decide to work quietly together, keeping a fairly low profile, until they are ready to move out towards their colleagues. But Kate's story (Chapter 3) offers a warning. Her group was lulled into a false sense of security by the degree of shared understanding that built up in the group and when it came to opening up to the rest of the staff Kate underestimated the gulf between the group and her other colleagues. Moreover, antagonism may build up as a result of suspicion about what a low profile group that meets on the school premises is up to – and rumour can compound anxiety and generate resistance that will block the group's progress when it does seek to extend its work. In the Castle School, members of the working party, although staunchly feminist in their personal lives, chose not to generate a feminist image for the group. It seems that groups that proclaim feminist credentials are still prone to misunderstanding, mockery or rejection, and a senior management team, unless its commitment and confidence are exceptionally strong, is unlikely to give backing to groups which threaten the semblance of cohesion which most schools need in order to continue functioning. The accounts remind us that gender leaders are not always starting from nothing. There may, for instance, be a history of past attempts to introduce work on gender that failed to confront practice at a whole-school level; or there may have been some individualised activities that faded when the teachers concerned left the school. The gender leaders may discover little pockets of committed but uncoordinated equal opportunities developments – individuals working on gender issues in the privacy of their own subjects or classrooms. In these circumstances, when some official or quasi-official move is made that legitimises work on gender – and is made by someone who is perceived as a potential ally – then the teachers involved may fairly readily be organised to spearhead a whole-school gender initiative.

Another point: in none of the schools whose work is reported here were the first steps towards a whole-school gender policy taken from a position of steady confidence but rather from a spirit of commitment and determination sharpened by a sense of potential vulnerability. The involvement and support of a genuinely concerned senior management team seems, in the end, to be a determining factor in the successful development of whole-school policy and practice.

A small but possibly important observation is that some schools avoided – unconsciously, perhaps, rather than by design – generating any obvious focus for dissent in their work on gender: there was therefore no 'talking point' around which the hostile could rally. This was certainly so at Castle School and was undoubtedly a feature of the successful passage of the various activities.

There is, in all the stories, an element of opportunism. The gender leaders were ready to harness whatever resources become available, both financial and human and whether from TVEI or from the LEA; they found out about small grants for special events such as International Women's Day, about theatre groups that offered performances on gender, about women writers and poets who would work in schools, about good speakers who could be trusted not to generate hostility on whole-school professional development days. They were willing to indulge in small-scale bribery, knowing that their colleagues would often be prepared to develop non-sexist texts if small amounts of money were available to buy time or materials. And they knew that, in the present market-place climate, getting good external publicity for the school will help colleagues to look favourably on new developments – as would having the testimony of ex-pupils or members of the community who have successfully pursued a career in an occupation where, traditionally, their gender would have been a deterrent.

And finally, to a lesser or greater extent, the teachers used evidence of unwitting but identifiable discrimination within the school as a basis for bringing in their colleagues.

The Castle School: a way in through International Women's Day

The Castle School is a 13–18 comprehensive with 800 pupils on role,[1] including 150 in the sixth form. Forty-five per cent of the population consists of pupils from ethnic minority groups: the largest group is Asian, the second largest Afro-Caribbean, and there are also numbers of Vietnamese and Chinese pupils. The school was formed in 1972 from an amalgamation of adjacent boys' and girls' grammar schools. The schools were separated by only a small internal yard and the timings of the school days were structured so that the pupils in the two schools never met during their breaks! One female member of staff who was appointed shortly after the amalgamation recalls how difficult it was for people to adapt: 'I was asked to spend breaks in a separate staff room to the men who were playing bridge and smoking'. Some ex-grammar school staff are still in post and there are undercurrents in the school – memories, comparisons with 'the good old days'. Another teacher who joined the school five years ago said this:

When I first came I couldn't stand the attitudes of a lot of people . . . Very little sympathy for children who had learning difficulties . . . A lot of people were harking back to the old days when it had been a prestigious grammar school . . . There were lots of comments – 'We're not getting good kids'.

Recently, however, this teacher has noticed a new spirit of commitment to change:

There has been a new head, other senior management changes and I love it now . . . There's so much going on and people are really beginning to address issues . . . We've got a long way to go but I do think that the general feeling of the staff is that we're working with the kids.

The new head has a strong commitment to comprehensive education. When he joined the school one of his priorities was to dismantle the separate remedial unit and withdrawal unit, develop more integrated structures, and establish a spirit and structure that signalled access and acceptance: 'We've come a long way. We're going in the right direction. But we're not there yet', he said.

Work in equal opportunities had been going for a year at the time of the fieldwork and was being coordinated by a working group. The focus of their planning was a major, whole-school gender launch, using International Women's Day as the vehicle. Before the working group was established there had been a number of new appointments – teachers who applied for jobs at the school because they wanted to teach in an inner city comprehensive. There was therefore a new wave of concern and commitment but there was not, as yet, an equal opportunities policy or real coordination of effort:

At the beginning it just seemed like there were well-intentioned people, pockets (of interest) in different areas, but nobody to draw the ideas together.

Sexist practices in the school were commented on by a member of the working party:

[There's been] sexism towards girls that hasn't been dealt with . . . The way that boys were allowed to talk to girls . . . Girls called all sorts of names . . . In this environment it seemed like it was going to be very difficult for girls to get positive images of themselves . . . Girls would shout back at boys but I never felt they were defending themselves as girls – it was just hurling abuse back . . . Books [had] boys as heroes and girls in limited roles. Men [on the staff] who sit in a group together and make derogatory comments – very sexist and very patronising towards women . . . whistling at women out of windows . . .

Several staff, including a member of the senior management team, also commented on the macho dimensions of the way that male pupils and some male staff expected disciplinary problems to be handled.

The equal opportunities group was set up by the senior management team. They appointed as chair of the group a woman whose strengths are knowing the school staff well, getting on with them all, and having an excellent capacity for informal support. She is also head of a department and, therefore, has some status in the formal structure of the school. She accepted the appointment and invited six other people to form a working party.

The members (I interviewed four) have an interesting range of positions and are, surprisingly perhaps, given the diversity of their starting points, striking in their agreement and mutual support. One described herself as joining because of her commitment to multi-ethnic education:

> My mother's South African and my father is very, very anti-racist. I've always had an interest in anti-racist activities and I've picked up on other issues – gender, disability, status – on the way. I found myself teaching in a nice middle class school but in the end I decided that I had to do something about what I felt and so when the job came up here I went for it.

Another member described herself as a strong feminist:

> I am actively involved in a number of things – oppression on all fronts, not just race and gender . . . I came here – I have only been here a year – because I wanted to work in a multi-racial school.

Gill, the group's chairperson, represents the middle ground:

> I feel that I am a feminist, but also I am not a feminist. I am a passionate believer in balance . . . I care very much about peoples' experiences, kids and staff, and believe that we should all find ways of getting on without causing casualties on the way. You two [addressing two fellow members of the group] have such strong and clear thoughts and views and sometimes I think I couldn't be like you, but I wish I could.

The group models in an excellent way the principle of 'getting on well together' and despite their different perspectives, they do fundamentally care about the same things.

The group describes itself as a think tank. They discuss their ideas with the senior management team (SMT), modifications may be suggested, but once an idea is agreed, there is reliable support from SMT in relation to resources, organisation and participation. Senior staff are also protective and do not allow the working group to become a scapegoat for any ill-feeling. Without taking the credit for the group's plans they try to emphasise that what is happening is important for the whole school. At the same time, the group has a sense that SMT could take the whole thing over: 'They could marshall us, muscle in on us, but I don't think they would'.

The group's attitude to their colleagues is also interesting. They note but are not prepared to be angered by the occasional jokey hostility, such as 'What about an International Man's Day then?', or, 'If women are organising anything, it's bound to fail'. Their tolerance pays off, it seems, and some colleagues who predicted failure for the school's International Women's Day event had the grace to acknowledge their mistake: 'I thought it would be a disaster but I was wrong'. Sceptics on the staff find themselves in the kind of informal discussion that Gill is particularly good at; when they say, 'I can't see what it's about. I can't see what the issue is', she spends time with them, believing that winning converts is important and has to be managed gently: 'It can't happen unless staff are convinced of its purpose and value'. Her responsibility, as she sees it, is to be 'aware of their reservations, not to attack them'.

The members of the group understand how difficult it is for many of their colleagues to see things differently and to change their habits – they are sympathetic but none the less strong in their conviction that for the sake of the students such colleagues must be helped to change. Gill commented: 'I honestly feel that most people do what they feel is right for the kids. Most people . . . We have to take them from where they are and move them along a bit'. 'What worries me', said another member of the working party, is the staff 'who are good teachers but who are underachieving because they feel that their styles, their attitudes and their values may be under attack; they feel that they don't have any currency any more'. These colleagues are seen, at some level, as victims, and the members of the group try to help them, as far as they can, to understand what equality is about and to feel that they can work effectively within a new framework if they are prepared to do some rethinking. Nevertheless, there is a bottom line: 'This is a professional issue and ultimately it's got to be equality for all, supported by all'. But they do not expect to succeed with all staff and recognise that the impending reorganisation within the LEA, which requires staff in secondary schools to reapply for jobs, may provide an opportunity for some staff to look for a post in a setting where the commitment to building a whole-school policy on equality that will genuinely guide practice is less advanced, or is less determined, than it is at this school. Meanwhile, those colleagues who were finding the work on gender uncongenial were quietly seeking solace in each other's company; they were not seen as constituting any real threat to the development of the work.

The working group decided then, in its first year of activity, to put all its efforts into one event – International Women's Day – and to use it as a way of signalling the school's commitment to working on gender: 'We latched onto it because we knew we could do it'. It had the advantage of being an event that was nationally recognised and it could not therefore be seen as a working party whim. The idea was to involve all the pupils in years 9, 10 and 11, with support from sixth formers, but in the event year 11 pupils missed out because of concern about GCSE. Organisationally it was challenging; 463 individual timetables were prepared which reflected individual choices from among a wide range of activities on offer.

There was some discussion about whether the event should be for girls only; as one member of the group said: 'I didn't want it to be about the boys – they get a lot every day', but her colleagues dissuaded her, arguing that both male students and male colleagues needed help in changing their attitudes. Individual members of staff were approached and asked to lead an activity, and personal networks were used to identify and bring in people from the locality. The day went extremely well, by all accounts. Staff and students enjoyed it. Feedback was good. There were some favourite moments: a group of boys – including an habitual truant – working with obvious enjoyment and a sense of responsibility in the creche; a bearded man seen singing softly to himself as he learned to knit. A video made by pupils with support from a women's video team recorded some of the highlights of the day. Importantly, the day enabled some teachers who had been quietly expressing their commitment to equality in their own classrooms to recognise and take advantage of a groundswell of support within their own staff.

The working group was realistic, however. It was a highly successful one-off event. It wouldn't change attitudes in itself but it effectively set the scene for further work. They went on to identify a number of things that the school might turn to next:

- an off-site inservice event, focusing on equality issues, for all staff;
- setting up, experimentally, some girls-only groups;
- undertaking some systematic monitoring of careers destinations, according to gender and ethnicity;
- monitoring the pattern of exclusions;
- organising a residential conference for year 10 pupils with pupils from a school for children with special needs;
- undertaking a curriculum audit which would focus on gender in relation to option choices, texts and teaching styles.

The working group, with support from the management team, made a start on the girls-only meetings: after a deliberately low key invitation to pupils in assembly, there were 12 volunteers. The girls and interested staff met first to watch a video made by the LEA of the different things that girls' groups had done elsewhere and then made their choices which included taster sessions on riding motorbikes, doing aerobics together, working on computers together, learning the basics of self-defence, and beginning to talk about their experiences as young women. Again, this was a matter of gently and successfully establishing precedents and opening up possibilities.

At the same time, the working party thought a lot about the justification for the other priorities that they had proposed. In relation to their concern to monitor exclusions, they commented:

We put a lot more energy into boys in that aspect of school life and that energy is not being put into girls – not that the boys don't need support and help, but it shows a vast difference in energy consumed which isn't being evenly distributed among boys and girls.

They had ideas about possible alternatives to exclusion but their first concern was to gather evidence so that their colleagues could see what was happening for themselves. They also gave thought to what needed to be done in relation to careers advice. The careers teacher was a member of the working group and she commented:

I suppose at the moment I'm treading this tightrope between sort of having some respect for the feelings of parents and not inviting them in to the careers interviews. I'm very aware that for Asian girls in particular [inviting in their parents] means maybe I'm actually removing some of their freedom to talk about what they'd like to do, where they see themselves going. What I try to do at the moment – it's very unsatisfactory – is to say to all pupils that if they want a separate interview they can have it . . . Not many take me up on that and it has often been black pupils, boys, who feel under pressure to follow certain career routes – professions, medicine, science – and they often don't want to do that.

At that time, the work experience placements showed that only one pupil in the year cohort had opted for a non-stereotypical placement. There was indeed a lot to do.

The members of the working group were still prepared to go gently forward, trying to take their colleagues with them: 'We should be talking and reasoning as well as challenging'; 'We don't want to go leaping in with both feet and alienating people'. Looking back on the first year's work, the chair of the working party said this: 'I feel that we're at the start of a very long road'.

The next nine months

From International Women's Day we've managed to get a whole-school project going. (LEA equal opps adviser)

A one-day event can only do so much in itself. But not only was the event successful, it generated debate and a readiness to go further within the school, it achieved good publicity for the school, and, importantly, it made the LEA equal opportunities team believe that this was a school that was worth investing in. The LEA had decided on a rolling programme of priorities, starting with equal opportunities and work with parents and the community, and money was available to help launch approaches that could be monitored and reported to other schools.

The school's own working group had already launched the first girls-only group as an after school, voluntary meeting and this paved the way for a larger, curricular initiative. Year 9 pupils were to be the main target in the hope that new perspectives and expectations could be established in the new cohort and carried through the rest of their school career.

In science and technology girls and boys were to be taught separately, with each group participating in activities that would stereotypically be regarded as more appropriate for the other group. Single sex groupings were also maintained for PSE where pupils' reactions to the groupings were discussed along with other gender-related issues. Teachers and advisers commented, in particular, on the discussions in PSE. They were 'astounded' by the depth of discussion and the strength of feeling expressed in the girls' groups. Some of the women who chaired them said they were 'the highlight' of their week. Staff were also very aware of the difficulty that the boys' groups had in opening up the issues; in the end the teachers working with them backed off discussion and gave the boys exercises where they could work more individually. Interestingly, a majority of boys indicated in the debriefing questionnaire that they would prefer to remain in single sex groups whereas girls – having got a lot off their chests, as some teachers interpreted it – were ready to return to the everyday reality of mixed groups. A member of the school's working group commented:

I think it's worth it just to give the girls an opportunity; the boys dominate so much of the curriculum and so much of what goes on in school. I see nothing wrong in giving girls a few weeks to have that space.

Another focus for the school was the system of options which, in the past, had shown strong stereotypical patterns. Year 10 pupils were consulted about the choices that they had made, what had influenced their choices, what they now thought of their choices, and what advice they would give to year 9 pupils. One finding was that pupils had not understood what was really entailed in some subjects if they had not studied them before. The school was already experimenting with an options poster which was radically revised in the light of the information from the survey. Further, the school discovered that some subjects, such as outdoor pursuits, had been chosen by significantly more girls after there had been an opportunity for active, single sex participation on the International Women's Day programme. The school also decided to give more thought to the nature of the counselling offered by form tutors.

At the same time, the LEA offered resources to support direct work with parents and local employers. The school is located right at the centre of a large city and pupils travel in from a number of different directions and areas. There is no clearly defined school 'community'. It is difficult therefore for the school to build up strong links with parents. The aim of the new activity was to encourage parents to come into school to discuss their children's futures. Experience has shown that when letters of invitation are sent home via pupils there is, quite often, a tendency for some letters to be forgotten or deliberately mislaid. The small grant from the LEA was spent on posting invitations to parents of year 9 pupils and translating them into four languages. The school was pleased with the the the impact: members of 77 families attended – a much higher proportion than usual. The disappointment was that only 8 Asian and Afro-Caribbean families attended – but, as the careers teacher said, 'Word will go round that the school has tried hard'. The evening was about gender and option/career choices. After a brief welcome, parents met in groups of not more than ten, each with a facilitator who was skilled in encouraging questions and discussion, a member of the careers service, and a teacher. Local FE representatives, employers, industrialists, advisers and community representatives were also present. One teacher recalled the anxiety of parents once they realised that they were to work in groups and not have the protection of being a member of an audience – 'but once in the groups, once the ice had been broken, everybody felt it was a useful way of doing things and appreciated the opportunity to talk'. The ice-breaking task was a variation on the well known 'Dennis and Denise' exercise where group members are given brief cvs of two young people but not told that one is a boy and one a girl; they project subject choices, career choices and futures – usually very different; they then see that the cvs are in fact identical and that the differences in the projections are related to preconceptions about gender.

Shortly after this event came the annual careers convention for year 10 pupils – jointly planned by four secondary schools and, this year, hosted by the Castle School. The convention lasted two days. Another small LEA grant gave the careers teacher four days release to plan and consult with participating employers and other schools. Rather than have the usual stands with representatives offering leaflets, the school decided to ask each employer to plan a 20 minute interactive event; observers sat in on every session and offered feedback, not only on the levels of participation but also on any evidence of gender discrimination. On the second day of the event those employers who had received criticism during the feedback session had made valiant efforts to improve, some totally redesigning their approach overnight. Again, the school was judged to have taken a bold and effective step in the right direction. A number of other events helped to sustain the momentum – including exchange visits with pupils from a special school and an off-site in-service day on equal opportunities for the whole staff.

Recognising the need for careful monitoring so that staff might know what the various initiatives were achieving, the LEA offered additional resources to allow an evaluative overview to be written jointly by the female deputy and an adviser for equal opportunities.

A member of the original working group commented on the way that the activities in the school had grown from the initial event – the celebration of International Women's Day:

It's taken off and you get that feeling that staff are very much aware of it even if they don't agree with it . . . Everybody knows what's happening and virtually every member of the staff has been involved in something . . . There's a hard core – I don't think it is changing them, but, yes, they accept it . . . I think there are a significant number of staff on the middle ground who maybe weren't committed from the outset but who are seeing interesting and exciting things happening and wanting to be involved . . . It's been handled very skilfully. There has been nothing very threatening – and also there's been no focus for the dissenters.

The LEA equal opportunities adviser who has been most closely involved seemed delighted with the progress:

What's smashing about this school is it won't rest, won't let it be pushed to one side . . . It's been really exciting working in this school because I've been able to go further than I've been in any other school . . . There's been a core of about ten very committed, very conscientious people ... There are people genuinely committed to equality throughout all the hierarchical structures. It's tremendous.

There are still new things to be done, of course. For instance, a male teacher sees the need for more work on discipline: 'When there are confrontations between male staff and young male students it often takes a very macho form – men have a lot to lose in public confrontations and I think there are other ways round than confrontation'. Another concern is for Asian girls: 'Some are going as far as A level because they're in the kind of positive and safer community of school and then, on leaving school, they're not actually doing anything else with their achievements'.

A cautionary note (although about equal opportunities and race rather than gender) came from a member of the working group anxious that in the euphoria of recent developments, some of the small contradictions between aspiration and current practice might be overlooked. She had recently encountered a black student in the corridor who was not attending his maths class: 'It turned out that he was slung out of his maths before Christmas and he is not going to sit any exams. He has been doing extra English all these weeks. He is a boy who has got plenty of skills. It's incidents like that that make you realise that there's lots of bits we haven't yet got on top of'.

The Forge School: a way in through achievement

If schools are not about achievement then I don't know what they are about. (headteacher, Forge School)

At the Forge School[2] work on gender is developing as part of the school's overall commitment to working on achievement. The head launched the drive on achievement and a recently appointed senior teacher, Sandy (now a deputy head), led the work on gender. The particular perspective on gender that she developed fitted well within the framework of concerns that the head, Michael, was addressing as a priority for the school.

In her previous school, Sandy and some of her colleagues had concentrated on developing a curriculum and structures that were fair to pupils from minority ethnic cultures but, she said, 'I had no awareness whatsoever of equal opportunities gender. Didn't see it as an issue at all. It wasn't there for me'. She was then seconded to her LEA to work as an advisory teacher in the TVEI team and alongside her main responsibility, which was for business studies, she was asked to take gender on board. She attended a three-day training programme – 'and that was the starting point. Since then it's just been like a big snowball. The minute the shutters started to rise – you know, it's just the more I see, the more I see. The more I become aware, the more inequities and problems I notice around me'. The training course had a distinctive line on gender: it accepted that in any institution there is likely to be a diversity of value positions in relation to equality issues and it presented working for equality as a *professional* responsibility – which involves looking closely at outcomes, hearing what stories the outcomes tell about what the school is doing for its pupils, and then taking professional action in the light· of those stories.

While she was able to argue for the professional line in school, it did not protect Sandy from the turbulence of reviewing her own circumstances and sense of self:

It's undoubtedly helped me to recognise that I have potential. By the time I'd got the TVEI job I was more than pleased that I'd got that far but it's given me more reliance on myself. It's been a difficult time for my family – we don't necessarily live an equal opportunities life as a family. At home I've chosen to opt out as far as my sons are concerned and it's been quite difficult for my husband. In some ways I'm an old-fashioned woman who still waits on the men and I don't confront that expectation all of the time. That's a decision that I made. But the whole family is more equal opps literate now!

The Forge School has 860 pupils on roll: 300 are entitled to free school meals; there are 80 sixth form pupils, with about 25 in each year taking A level courses. Approximately 11 per cent of pupils are from minority ethnic cultures; the largest groups are Sikh and then Hindu, with a few Muslim families, some Vietnamese and some Chinese families. Indeed, when Sandy joined the school as senior teacher, she found that the head had already initiated some work on race and had appointed an Asian home-school liaison tutor. The school also had section 11 funding. Much less had been done on gender although there had been a few individual, and relatively contained, initiatives. For instance, there was a small equal opportunities group within the science department which produced some recommendations but the group 'fell by the wayside when one of its main members went off on secondment'. Another initiative was taken by the head of lower school who set up a group of local primary school deputy heads whose brief was to look at gender:

It didn't get very far, largely because there were different perceptions within the group. Some saw themselves as classroom teachers rather than as managers and the group didn't gell. It produced a document which addressed things like not having children line up in two lines, having the names mixed on the register, being aware of boys taking up all the playground space with girls stood on the sidelines, and so on. So they had this document but they didn't go back into the schools and manage the change.

So gender 'died a death' but the group decided that it wanted to go on meeting and took as its enthusiastic focus 'traditional playground games' which, the head of lower school acknowledged, was a topic whose historical interest was likely to swamp any concern with gender.

Sandy attempted to offer a strong, school-wide definition to the concerns of interested individuals and link them into a concerted plan of action. As a fellow teacher said, 'Sandy very much had the idea that we needed to build equal opportunities on something concrete so they started looking at exam results'. 'They' were the members of a gender group that Sandy set up. She went about identifying the members of this group with great care:

Gender is often perceived in schools as 'a woman's problem'. And often it gets held up because it's initiated by women and very often by low status women. To make progress for the school you have to access the power even if that power's held by men. That's the reality of the situation and to ignore it would be foolhardy.

Sandy waited a term before talking to people about joining the group so that she could 'get a feel for the staff'. She wanted people who were influential in themselves, both men and women, and she also wanted to reflect a range of formal status positions: 'I wanted some enthusiasts – I wanted some good solid support; I was also quite happy to take one or two sceptics but not too many because we didn't want to get held up at too early a stage'. She also wanted some representation of subject areas that were traditionally problematic in terms of gender. She drew in a head of technology – 'I had to do an awful lot of hard selling to get him on. He was holding me at arm's length because he'd got national curriculum coming, too many things to do, but he was persuaded and now he's one of the most active people in the group'. There was also a science teacher, the head of home economics, a PE teacher, a geography teacher, the careers officer, and a new English teacher. The group met three times a term in their own time. Sandy commented: 'It's a very enthusiastic group. There's nearly always full attendance. It's only very pressing things that keep people away'. Two sixth formers were also invited to join the group, one male and one female, to offer a pupil perspective.

Once the group was chosen Sandy went for a brisk, businesslike start:

I didn't actually invite any discussion. I said that our starting point is that we as a professional body of staff believe that youngsters should not be disadvantaged because of gender or race.

There was one occasion, Sandy recalls, 'where discussion focused for a time on personal and home factors and it started to fall apart. People started challenging each other and debating and I had to intervene very quickly. Our basic belief has to be that as professionals we shouldn't disadvantage youngsters and I tried get the group to stick with that idea'. The group started on something that Sandy presented as 'absolutely directly attributable to the school' – the exam results: 'If they're not the product of the work that we've done with our pupils, well . . .' Sandy explains why she took this line:

One of the problems that I've seen in other schools is that equal opportunities work can be divisive. A lot of the recommendations revolve around people's daily practices, the way they interact with youngsters in the classroom, the way administration is carried out in the school. And when attention is drawn to these things people can feel that they're being criticised. They feel defensive. Then what happens is you don't ever get to the heart of what's going on. It doesn't touch the things that are important.

Sandy had not been impressed by schools that adopted the easygoing, liberal-sounding approach where teachers say, 'Nobody's stopping the girls doing technology. It's there if they want it'. The rhetoric can sound warm, says Sandy: 'You put some posters on the wall, you give the girls a talk and then you leave them to respond' but something tougher is needed to begin to combat the sexism that structures the responses of so many female and male pupils. Sandy favoured an approach where teachers try to work directly on something that is closely related to achievement. The obvious starting point was the analysis of examination results – equality of outcome. In order to get some sense of what the school does for its pupils, Sandy needed some base-line data but the only measure of pupils' 'level' at entry to the school was the Verbal Reasoning Quotient. Some staff were not entirely happy with that but hoped that the national curriculum programme of testing would offer a more appropriate baseline for the future.

Sandy's training had offered a model for working on GCSE results: first, a 'picture' of a particular subject area is built up, some possible hypotheses that might explain the 'picture' are constructed, and the hypotheses plus the data are circulated to all departments as a stimulus to reflection on their own patterns of results. Sandy's colleagues wanted to modify the approach; instead, they invited departments to take on for themselves the task of analysing their exam results using a framework of 'expected' and 'actual' achievement. An arc of acceptable deviation was drawn above and below each grade and if the pupil performed outside that 'arc of expectation' then she or he was judged to have over- or under-achieved. A summary of the patterns of over- and under-achievement is then circulated to all staff, discussed within departments and followed-up through discussion with members of the senior management team. The aim is to get staff in all departments to say to themselves: 'Is this what's happening?' and then to start asking, 'Why is it happening?' As Sandy said: 'You can't get a totally clear picture because there are so many factors to unravel but we're beginning to see better what the areas of concern are'.

The first exercise, carried out on the 1989 GCSE results, showed, for instance, that the pattern of pupils who were not entered for examinations was gender-related and that boys' weakness in coping with the requirements of course work was a factor in both under-achievement and non-entry. The exercise also revealed some of the dimensions of under-achievement. Take science, for instance: the school's analysis suggested that approximately half the pupils were under-achieving in one science subject – in short, as Sandy said, 'Science is failing our pupils; it's certainly failing our girls but it's also failing a fair proportion of our lads'. Departments have done well to accept the scheme because, as Sandy pointed out, 'Although we've tried to handle it as sensitively as possible, it can be threatening to have to acknowledge departmental figures publicly'. But the threat was softened by a recognition among the staff as a whole that the school needed to do everything it could to raise pupils' aspirations and achievements. The important next step, of course, is to help individual departments consider what particular action they can take to respond to the findings.

The school's overall action plan for achievement has focused on options and attendance as priorities. An early commitment was to try to ensure that in subsequent years all information – options choices, attendance patterns, examination results, and post-16 destinations – is kept in an accessible form and is broken down by gender, ethnicity and social class.

It appeared that there had been some concern in the school for some years about the options procedures:

It used to be organised and run by a longstanding member of staff who recently retired. That person wasn't particularly equal opps minded and was a believer in jobs for the boys and jobs for the girls. So with him leaving there was a lot of thinking and discussion.

A deputy head prepared an analysis showing the number of boys and girls choosing each of the school's options and also the number who changed their minds during the process: 'There were some strange things happening': for instance, three times as many boys as girls were choosing geography, and in technology four times as many boys as girls changed their minds after initially opting for a particular option (i.e., boys were moving away from food technology which was still seen by some as 'cooking'). Sandy and the group set up a small-scale research project and 15 pupils were interviewed – 'just too small a sample to give us real conclusions but it did flag up some of the things that we needed to address'. These included the fact that both boys and girls lacked real understanding of what the subjects were that they were opting for; the fact that parents had greater influence on option choices than staff had anticipated; and the fact that subjects had strong 'characters' so that history was seen as about people and was therefore attracting more girls while geography was seen as more impersonal and seemed, for this reason, to be attracting more boys. Interestingly, the interviews also showed that preferences for particular teachers did not figure as largely as staff thought they would.

The interview with a small number of pupils was succeeded the following year by a questionnaire given to all pupils to try to find out more about the basis for choice. In addition, a group of pupils thought to be at risk was targetted for special counselling; a review of teachers' practices in setting homework regularly was undertaken and a home-work room was subsequently provided on the school premises for pupils who found it difficult to find a quiet space to get on with their work at home.

Alongside the work on options, Michael, the head, was launching a systematic and regular review of attendance. The blitz on attendance started with an inset day which gave staff a chance to discuss strategies before starting an action programme the following September. Teachers explained to pupils about the need for attendance, cumulative figures for individual forms were calculated as the basis for an incentive scheme, and the head undertook a detailed analysis which allowed him to make comparisons with similar weeks during the preceding year: 'I plot it, monitor it, and we ask questions about it', he said. Attendance figures went up by about 5 per cent for every week of the year as a result of the drive – which represents 'an additional 3,000 pupil days per term'. Parents were brought into the scheme for promoting attendance and they knew that unexplained or continuing absenteeism would be followed-up. As the head said: 'If you've got a youngster who says in the morning, "I've got a bit of a headache. I don't think I'll go to school", in this area you're likely to give into that pressure, but if you know you're going to have the school on your back, then you have to think which pressure is the greater.'

The Forge School is, as we have seen, concerned with examining the scaffolding for pupil achievement. Part of this scaffolding, alongside attendance, options and examination entries and outcomes, is aspirations post-16. The school is keen to encourage more young people to continue with full-time education but this is a tough assignment given local habits – as the head of sixth form studies explained:

In this area they tend to go for jobs without training . . . So we have to sort of re-educate them into thinking more of a career as opposed to a job . . . It's not an area where families will automatically think about continuing with education – and higher education is even further from their thoughts. There are very few parents of children with a background of higher or further education.

The head explained that it's even difficult to get parents – and sometimes the pupils – to understand, or remember, that an A level course lasts two years.

The locality is, it seems, one that quickly shows the marks of recession. As the head said:

We've lost a lot of jobs in the area and I think that's partly because the economy locally is not underpinned with training in modern industry . . . So a big priority would be to increase the aspirations of the whole community and help them to see why investment in training is needed.

There are a number of parents who work on markets or who have small family firms and so there are openings for pupils who want to go into the family business. The boundaries of the area seem to be closely defined and people do not seek jobs too far away. Indeed, even on work placements the expectation of parents is that the pupil will not be required to travel far: 'If he's got to go on a bus he's not going'. As the head of sixth said: 'Families here don't take easily to change. It's going to be a slow process'. And a deputy head added: 'If we can see how to turn the fathers around then I think I could change the world! I think the mothers on the whole tend to be a little bit more receptive to change . . . The fathers are far more ingrained, particularly in their gender roles'. These perspectives clearly influence the way young people think about their futures:

In the past the girls very much thought that their destination was as home-makers. And the boys very much saw themselves as macho wage earners . . . The situation in this part of the world has actually helped change that because we've reached a situation where men don't find employment so easily and therefore the mums have had to go out to work and that has caused many problems in the home but the spin-off is that the children see their mums working and more girls and boys are now saying they would expect to share roles in the family. (deputy head)

The school has an annual 'Equal People Day' when men and women from the region who are working in non-stereotypical jobs spend a day in the school talking with year 9 pupils. The day is organised as part of a new 5-week module on equal opportunities which aims, before pupils make their option choices, to 'widen their perceptions and aspirations in relation to the world of work and to try and break down some of the stereotypes concerning jobs and roles.' The event that I attended brought together 18 people from the region who were all pursuing non-stereotypical careers: the participants included two women who were working, as buyer and surveyor respectively, on construction sites; a male nursery nurse; a female senior executive officer in accountancy; a disabled sports development officer; a female carpenter. A third of the participants were black. The new module culminates in an exercise where pupils are able to role play discussing with their parents possible option choices and careers.

The school's relationship with local employers seems to be prospering. The school is involved in an industry consortium which involves approximately 25 placements a year in fairly unusual job settings. The school has also participated in a national competition sponsored by the Girls into Science and Technology Initiative where pupils were invited to make their own videos. One, made at Forge School and highly commended, showed 'this really very attractive, bubbly woman who'd just got a first class honours in engineering; it was saying to girls, "Look. If you want to go into engineering, don't think you've got to have male characteristics or that you're always going to look grubby in dirty overalls"'. The image was very much of the successful woman.

There are also signs that some local employers are themselves beginning to take the issues of access for women seriously. For instance, recognising that the pace of technological change is so rapid, one local firm is ensuring that women who are on maternity leave do not become deskilled and they are being provided with computers at home so that they can keep up their skills.

Secondary schools in this local authority double as community colleges (although the authority as a whole does not have a particularly radical policy for adult access to continuing education). There are many women with young families who worked as clerks or secretaries some years ago and who feel now that 'the doors are closed because they haven't got the skills':

In an ideal world they might be able to come here and do something as part of our business systems course but they can't unless they can make arrangements for their children to be cared for whilst they're here.

Some local authorities have tried to encourage mothers to upgrade their skills by providing creches at school sites. That doesn't happen here. One of the deputy heads outlined the need:

I have a young woman studying for an A level. On Mondays her mother looks after her children and she comes to my class. But on Thursdays she is not able to do this and so she can't attend.

Interestingly, one of the school's feeder primaries has an extended-day nursery attached to it and this gives mothers or single parent fathers greater opportunity to work or to study for further qualifications.

Penny, a woman in her late forties, is a striking example of what women can achieve. She is now manager of the export branch of a large local firm and regularly contributes to school-industry events. She explains how women can win through if they aim high and persevere:

I left school at 15. Started in an office at the bottom and worked my way up. I was an asthmatic in a family that prided itself on being healthy and everyone assumed that I would live the life of a semi-invalid. My mother was old-fashioned and saw 'work' as a physical thing and that didn't appeal to me. So I had a lot to prove to myself and everyone. I kept changing jobs, improving my position – and I didn't have any further education at that stage. I got married and had a child. By the time she was three I was ready to crawl up the wall I was so bored. And when I went back to work I'd not only lost my status but also my confidence. I worked as a temp for five years and that got me into the swing of things. Then I joined a local firm and stayed with it. After some years I was offered my present job. Then, with the changes in the business world and the recession I thought, well, I've enjoyed where I've got to and there's not a great deal of space for me to go further. But then I thought, 'No. I won't give up trying. If I had to move on for any reason it would be nice to say I'd recently done this and achieved that.' So I've come back to school and I'm doing a course in business studies and getting some more qualifications.

My husband's been very supportive but he was unemployed for over a year. When I was going to work one morning he came out on the front step to say cheerio, and he said, 'I never thought I'd be a kept man'. He's got a job again now – but I didn't realise how hard he took it when I was the only one earning.

I think a lot of young people should be encouraged to do jobs that aren't stereotyped. I don't believe in jobs for women and jobs for men. Having said that, it's still difficult trying to get on out there in a man's world.

The particular approach that the Forge School is pursuing, through its emphasis on access for all and outcomes for all, allows staff to review which pupils are losing out in different areas of school life and activity. While much of the concern will inevitably be for girls because, by and large, in the traditional structures of schooling they have missed out more than boys have done, where the evidence suggests that boys are also losing out the school is trying to be equally responsive. The staff are aware, for instance, that many boys are underachieving and that some of the underachievers are disaffected; when in school they can be disruptive and attention-seeking in ways that further disadvantage girls who can suffer because so much teacher time is being devoted to sub-duing the unruly behaviour of the disaffected boys. The school is not, therefore, vulnerable to the criticism that equality is 'only about the girls'.

St. Benet's School: a way in through the curriculum

The story of equal opportunities at St Benet's[3] is not so much about strategy as supported growth. Equal opportunities work developed and expanded in a seemingly 'natural' and free-flowering way, with work in drama in particular providing a reference point. The originator was Jenny – an assistant English/drama teacher (who later became head of department) and whose last job was in an all-boys' school where her commitment to equal opportunities issues sharpened her awareness. She and her colleagues had already been developing units of work in drama for younger pupils that focused on issues to do with bullying and adolescent friendships and Jenny was keen to extend the work to other topics and to other pupils in the school. Her determination to work for equal opportunities coninicided with an initiative of the LEA which invited schools to bid for money to support the beginnings of equal opportunities work in schools. Jenny wrote a proposal on behalf of the school and the school received some money to help it to take its first steps towards a long-term goal of producing an equal opportunities policy.

With the support of the deputy heads, Jenny set up a working group. Heads of departments were informed and the idea was generally well received. Since there was no requirement that every department be represented, the people who joined were volunteers from departments that welcomed the initiative and, in some cases, had already embarked on exploratory work in a small and private way. The group consisted, therefore, of keen, like-minded people whose departments were behind them. A drama teacher had already been working with colleagues from other schools on developing equal opportunities teaching materials and she joined the group, together with a sociology teacher who saw her subject as helping students engage with serious contemporary issues such as equal opportunities. A history teacher joined partly because she and Jenny shared an interest in local politics and were committed to issues of equality and justice. Another teacher joined because her department, modern languages, was concerned about the imbalance of numbers of male and female students at GCSE and at A level.

The group members set themselves the task of seeing what could be achieved within a term – the autumn term – and agreed to report back to each other in December. Work was carried out with energy and commitment and approaches were different in each department.

The English and drama departments developed units of work on prejudice, and the issues explored in role play and text were discussed at length in the regular feedback sessions. A year 9 drama group started a project on gender stereotyping; where normally a project lasts about three weeks, here the engagement of the pupils was such that the project extended over nine weeks. It included work on 'a woman's typical day', and it included the reversal of stereotypical roles (for instance, pupils presented women as football supporters, there was a sketch about a male beauty queen and another about a female pilot). Teachers were struck by the creativity of the groups, by their wit and by their commitment. Later in the year a drama consultant was invited in for a day to work with the year 9 pupils on gender issues and he commented after his visit:

Of the 250 or so schools I have visited throughout the UK, this is one of five in which the pupils have a heightened awareness of gender stereotyping and have the confidence to challenge sexism.

Again, video was used to record some of the pupils' work in drama and extracts were put together to help teachers in other schools think about the role of drama in opening up issues of gender equality.

In English, work on gender led to a review of the school's banding system. Teachers chose a short, scripted drama about a woman who had experienced prejudice. They brought together high-band and low-band pupils and constructed working groups of five (some from each band). The task was to assign roles, to read the play aloud and to discuss the issues. Pupils were then asked to write about the issues – and, later, the experience of working in mixed-band groups. The results were described as 'devastating'! Teachers commented in a written document:

In subsequent discussion and written work numerous accounts of personal suffering emerged as pupils described how the banding system in the school had nurtured prejudice amongst pupils and had damaged personal friendships and self-esteem . . . Perhaps the most satisfying aspect of the work was the evident change many pupils seemed to have experienced. Many of them expressed in their assignments that they now had a much greater understanding of how prejudice arose and were determined that they would be very careful to avoid causing pain to others by holding a prejudiced view. For those pupils who had been in the lower band, there was a realisation that they were not inferior to pupils in other bands. Pupil–pupil relationships improved as did pupil–teacher relationships.

Thus, the first term's work had some far-reaching effects – not the least in encouraging the school to move more generally towards a system of mixed ability teaching. The school also benefited from the positive publicity it received through the various initiatives and the attention of teachers in other schools.

Staff in the modern languages department did two things: they undertook a statistical analysis of pupil option choices nationally and compared them with recent statistics in their own school; they reflected the national trend which showed a decline in boys opting for modern languages. However, the national curriculum was seen as offering an opportunity to re-emphasise the value of modern languages in the new European society and, consequently, of changing the image of the subject. Staff also undertook two other enquiries. One involved looking at sexist images and language in text books and teaching materials and the other, an observation-based study, focused on interactions within modern languages lessons. The observation study produced a number of interesting findings that were followed up. It showed, for instance, how a year 9 high-band German class was taking 'a rather superior attitude towards others in their year' and was organised in separate and highly competitive single sex sub-groups. In the same year group, pupils in a mixed ability class studying another language were seen to be 'much more cooperative and supportive of each other'. In a year 11 class, where the girls outnumbered the boys by three to one, the boys were still dominant and the girls deferred to them. It was also discovered that parental pressure against boys taking modern languages at A level was quite strong.

The history department decided to concentrate on ways of promoting positive views of women in history. They briefed their pupils to conduct an analysis of text books and found that both boys and girls worked well together on the task and with great intellectual drive; the search for gender bias in texts subsequently became common practice in history. Where discrimination in textbooks, videos and other materials was found, instead of abandoning the teaching materials – which the school could not easily afford to do – the department used the materials as the basis for a critical discussion of omission and distortion. The department reviewed its syllabus, ensuring 'that every history topic includes women's roles': they looked at such things as the laws of inheritance which exemplify the oppression of women and they also planned a 'women's history fortnight', with materials offered by local libraries. Teachers in the department already felt strongly about equality and they were, in a sense, waiting for this opportunity to develop their work more fully. The following extracts are from a departmental working document:

The children in an all-white school are just as much victims of racism as children in a more mixed environment. We do not know where our pupils will eventually live or work and we feel that the history department can play a role in ensuring that they have at least a degree of tolerance in their attitude to others . . . historical writers have long pointed out that 'written history is the propaganda of the victor'. Victors have traditionally been white male and middle or upper class. Hence the diet of history as 'kings, dates and battles' . . . Archaeological evidence now suggests that stone age women were involved in many and varied tasks, not least of which were hunting and gathering to provide 80 per cent of the food required . . . In the Roman period it was considered quite common for women to lead armies and in the Saxon period women bought and sold property in their own right. Information like this is, however, only available in specialised texts. . . . A general examination of school text books reveals that women are either invisible and underrepresented or frequently represented inaccurately.

New projects were to be developed for year 9 options, each of which had a strong gender/justice framework, and opportunities for building on these concerns were identified in the GCSE syllabus.

The sociology teacher, since she had no departmental colleagues, decided to invite her sixth form students to investigate equality of opportunity in the school. They constructed a survey of GCSE examination entries and passes, and analysed the data along a gender dimension. They also planned a lesson for a year 8 class on challenging stereotypes, using role play as a key strategy, and their lesson, trialled with pupils in their own school, was video-recorded. The video was shown at a local conference on gender and teachers from some other schools invited the sixth formers to teach the lesson to pupils in their schools. At the same time, the teacher and her students undertook a review of fiction and non-fiction books in the library and funds were subsequently allocated to increase the stock of material relating directly to equal opportunities. They also produced a folder, for use by staff and students, with information on equal opportunities, including book lists, addresses of organisations, etc.

A way was found of displaying all the new teaching materials and communicating the high level of interest among pupils and the quality of their response. Drama was particularly useful here as a medium of communication for other staff and pupils. The gender work in drama was clearly yielding a high level of engagement and understanding which other departments could build on in their own curriculum work with pupils. It was also proving powerful as a means of presenting familiar situations in ways that enabled participants and audience to see the issues from a different perspective. Performances were put on for pupils outside the year 9 drama group:

> There was the most wonderful scene where the 'master of the house' came home from work and his wife was very subservient. He ordered her around and she had to bring him a drink and she came in on her hands and knees. And then the girl who played the housewife sat in a chair and just talked about her life and how she felt and the boredom and the fear and the way she hated being dominated but felt there was no way out.

Drama, which had been a popular option, was now made compulsory for all year 9 pupils and the work on bullying and friendship in years 7 and 8 was modified to lead into the new unit on gender and prejudice in year 9.

Drama was also the centrepiece of the first staff inset day on equal opportunities: 'I'd say the majority received it well. Some accepted it. Some were thankful it had been brought out into the open. Some treated it as a joke. And a few rejected it out of hand and thought it was a complete and utter waste of time'.

The work continued to grow in each participating department – sustained by the excitement it was generating:

> All of us in the department had other commitments, heavy teaching loads, meetings and yet, astonishingly, we were so enthused by our pupils' responses – they saw the issues as directly relevant to themselves – that we found time to discuss our successes and failures, to modify our materials, and to be supportive to each other.

Other departments joined the group as individual staff became interested and were prepared to take the lead. The first was the science department – through the recently appointed female head of biology who had a strong personal commitment to gender equality. She was particularly concerned about opening up career prospects for girls (as well as for low-achieving boys):

> The thing that strikes me is the year 11 girls – when they're leaving, an awful lot of them don't think of anything other than hairdressing, things like that. So I took five lessons and looked at careers in science but really it was just too little and too late ... A lot of girls are very good at science and get good grades but don't even consider any sort of job that might involve science – [they say] science, industry – that's difficult. I couldn't possibly work there.

Pupils, she said, 'have no conception of women being scientists in the real world', and so she organised work visits to places where both boys and girls could see young women engaged in scientific/industrial activities. She talked about the difference between 'the comfort of the classroom' which helps some girls to feel confident and to begin to think about alternative careers and the tension they can experience if they then go home and try to fight against 'stereotyped opposition'. 'What we do in the school is minuscule compared with what they have learned since they were young,' she said, but nonetheless she works hard to ensure that the texts used in the science department offer images of women as contributors to the advancement of scientific knowledge.

The way that equal opportunities is developing at St Benet's reflects something of the structure of the school. It is a large school (1200 pupils) with over 70 staff. The lower school is on a separate site. There is no tradition of whole-staff meetings; instead, developments proceed through special panels which, as a matter of principle, include senior and more junior staff, men and women. St Benet's is a Roman Catholic Comprehensive in an area where secondary education is provided in a range of settings: in single-sex grammar schools, independent schools, comprehensive schools with and without sixth forms, RC maintained and aided schools, a sixth form college and an FE college. Twenty five per cent of the St Benet's pupils are from particularly disadvantaged backgrounds and the school suffers from creaming. For instance, pupils in Catholic primary schools commonly sit the 11 plus and if they pass they go to the RC aided grammar school; if they 'fail' they either pay fees or go to the RC comprehensive – St Benet's. Nevertheless, the school claims that it is doing well for its ablest children and at the time of the fieldwork two sixth form girls had won places at Oxford and Cambridge.

The head has a strong commitment to the comprehensive ideal: he regrets that schools that were once established to serve the poor are now catering for the rich and are marketing notions of privilege. St Benet's has a reputation for accepting pupils on transfer who have educational or behavioural difficulties – even though, in the present climate, such a reputation can lead parents to underestimate the school's concern for academic success.

There is in the school a fundamental commitment to each child's right of access and to her or his right to achieve. As the head says:

I want pupils to leave with skills but I also want them to leave with compassion and to leave knowing what the big issues are: population resources, environment, war and tyranny, the tyranny of materialism, and the complacency of Western and of affluent societies who pay lip service to democracy.

These are not easy aims for a school to take on in this region of the country which is renowned for macho, sport-dominated images of masculinity. Issues of equity in the curriculum and in the structure and relationships of the school are an expression of what the head describes as 'the humanity of the soul'.

In terms of school organisation the head aspires to 'unity' rather than to 'uniformity' – hence, perhaps, the way that departments are encouraged to translate principles into practice in their own ways, and hence the way that the whole-school equal opportunities policy grows organically through interested departments and through the display and celebration of the achievements of those departments.

Jenny and the members of the original equal opportunities group had agreed that they should not address 'those areas that might arouse strong dissent' among colleagues and they opted therefore for 'achievable targets' in their own curriculum areas. Their line of appeal to colleagues is that equal opportunities is an expression or enhancement of the school's concern 'to give all learners the chance to realise their full potential'; work on gender is about removing some of the barriers that often 'prevent a child from aspiring beyond narrow expectations'. Equal opportunities extends concern for the pupil's rights as an individual to the pupil as a member of a group that might be discriminated against on grounds of gender, race or class.

What the equal opportunities initiative is doing is to fill in some of the detail of the vision at the level of curriculum content and classroom interaction. It is a way of helping colleagues to uncover some of the inevitable contradictions in the small print of their practice (for instance, the strict differentiation by gender of dress in PE). Even so, not everyone has wanted to examine their practice, nor have they seen their priorities, at a busy time and with the national curriculum on the doorstep, as inevitably lying in the area of gender and equal opportunities. Jenny recalled her naivete in expecting that all women on the staff would want to become involved and that all male colleagues would be reluctant. Responses were in fact much less predictable.

It is interesting to consider the risks inherent in different approaches to building a whole-school commitment to equality. In schools where central coordination is strong and clearly defined, then the introduction of an up-front commitment to equality can lead to alienation or to the kind of confrontation that can be damagingly divisive. Here, at St Benet's, a de-centred approach and relatively loose coordination is customary – and here the risk is a possible loss of pace and/or lack of impact or take-up across the curriculum as a whole. But it may be that sustaining the rigorous achievements of the departments currently involved would be a more prudent strategy than trying to extend the active commitment to other departments. The departments involved so far have been remarkably successful in their work with pupils (as a recent HMI report also recognised) and there is, within the school, a framework of values that ensures that a commitment to gender equality will not be contested or undermined. It may be that in quieter times (after the upheaval of the upper and lower school amalgamation onto a single site, and when the national curriculum settles into a more comfortable normality) other interested individuals may bring their curriculum areas into the gender frame.

Note

1 I spent five days in the school over the space of a year and interviewed three members of the senior management team (2 on 2 occasions), 4 members of the equal opportunities working group (2 on 2 occasions) and six other members of staff. A colleague attended the whole of the second International Women's Day. I also interviewed the equal opportunities adviser who was most closely involved with the school.

2 I spent three days in the school interviewing Sandy (a deputy) and the head (each on two occasions), eight other members of staff, and some pupils. I also talked with a business woman from a local firm, an LEA adviser, who discussed the gender work in the school, and I attended and participated in one of the school's Equal People Days.

3 I spent three days in St Benet's School over the space of a year. I talked with groups of staff and pupils and interviewed the head and deputies (on two occasions) and seven other staff (some on two occasions). I studied curriculum materials produced by the school, and I also talked with the adviser for equal opportunities and a teacher who came in from a special needs school to support staff in working on behavioural problems.

5 DEVELOPING A WHOLE-SCHOOL POLICY

> Ultimately the way to understand something as complex as a
> school is probably to attempt to change it, since the change
> attempts, as they encounter blocks, facilitators or linkages . . .
> will reveal the complexity of the institution.
>
> (Reynolds 1984: 301)

Reynolds' observation is certainly confirmed by Townley School's
attempts to develop a whole-school gender policy.

The Townley School started to build its equality programme virtually
from scratch. The male deputy inherited the responsibility as part of
his job specification – and he was eager to take it on. He also inherited
an inert collection of materials – a symbol of bureaucratic compliance
– but no evidence that the thinking had really moved much beyond the
problem of filing the various equal opportunities documents. The nettle
had not been grasped: the documents made no fuss – the staff might.
And, when the new deputy got things going, some of the staff did
make a fuss.

Harry, the deputy, was fully supported by the head and by senior
colleagues. What motivated them was not a commitment to radical
feminist principles but rather a strong sense of the multiple disadvantage
that their pupils experienced – and a feeling that here was one layer
of disadvantage that the school might be able to help young people
do something about. It could try to build up more confident and
articulate aspiration among both girls and boys, but particularly among
the girls.

The initiative on gender was launched at a time of considerable
turmoil – some pressures were coming into the school from outside
(national curriculum planning, in particular) but some stemmed from

internal needs (the school was moving from two sites onto one, for instance, and was trying to fight for the continuation of its small sixth form). In one sense, this general busy-ness camouflaged the equality initiative – it didn't stand out too starkly – but on the other hand, it could the more easily be ditched. It wasn't ditched. The senior staff kept it going – richer or poorer, in sickness and in health.

A critical moment was the appointment of two new deputies – both women. The immediate, unguarded response of some groups on the staff was useful in that it exposed the extent to which women's disadvantage was not understood.

The work of this school is, I think, worth documenting because it is a story of ordinary struggle. The differences among the teachers emerged as an interestingly complex feature of the struggle. Those who were most ready to participate and signal their support had very varied perspectives on the equality issue. Other teachers had not thought about the issue or had felt it was not something that schools should become too involved in – it hadn't been an issue in the past:

> Each of us carries around those growing-up places, the institutions, a sort of backdrop or stage set. So often we act out the present against the backdrop of the past, within a frame of perception that is so familiar, so safe, that it is terrifying to risk changing it even when we know our perceptions are distorted, limited, constricted by that old view.
>
> (Orner 1992: 86)

Many teachers were ambivalent and they handled their ambivalence in different ways. But after the watershed of the appointment of the new female deputies there was no time when the opposition seemed strong enough to undermine the equality initiative.

Perhaps the most disturbing aspect of the struggle was the fact that some teachers were sceptical about their pupils' capacity to become more confident about themselves and their futures. It is easy for such teachers to style themselves the 'realists' in contrast to the 'romantics'. 'Realists' tend to invoke the cultural deprivation principle and in so doing set a boundary to what a school can achieve. In one sense they are right – the problems need to be tackled at the level of the deep structures of class inequality, but there are still things that the school can do. As Whyld says, 'Working within the system does not mean giving up the fight to change it' (1983: 297; quoted by Weiner 1986: 272).

Key features of the approach in this school include the attempt to build consistency of purpose and practice across a number of fronts;

the structuring of the equal opportunities working party around departmental representation – one dimension of coverage; the status of an
agreed policy statement and the responsibility of the senior management
team to make sure that the principles it embodies are respected; a
concern to help pupils talk about equality issues and to reflect on them
in different situations; and a gradual feeding in of other equality concerns, race and disability, for instance. The school had not yet worked
out what it might do with parents – other than make sure that they
knew about the policy and that the key phrases were clear and easy to
remember.

The account underlines the importance of determined support on the
part of senior staff. As Corson (1992: 249) says:

> For values of justice to really count, they need to be inserted into
> the discourse of the place; they need to be articulated sincerely
> by significant figures in the organisation so that they become
> part of the taken-for-grantedness of the place.

It also suggests that the commitment must indeed be 'sincere' for it is
the commitment that, in the end, has to keep the initiative alive. There
are no national awards for work on equality and no great material
inducements. The school knew that its local equal opportunities adviser,
who was very committed, thought highly of what they were doing
but the rewards are largely professional and intrinsic – hearing pupils
talk differently about themselves and their futures and thinking that
you are, perhaps, making a difference.

The Townley School

The school

Townley School opened as a comprehensive in the 1950s. It had a
differentiated structure – including a 'grammar' and a 'technical' band,
which was retained until the mid-1980s when a new head tried to create
a climate and structure in which all pupils would have equal access to
the same curriculum. At the same time the number of pupils on roll
had fallen and there had to be some loss of staff: 'It was like the surgeon's
knife: it cut out the past and set up the future. He got it going in the
right direction but it unnerved the staff' (current deputy). A little later,
money for professional development available through the Government's In-Service (GRIST) Initiative helped 'to heal the wounds, to get
teachers talking and thinking'. The head who had initiated the changes,
after only a short period in office, left the school. A fairly recently

appointed deputy took over – and was ultimately appointed as head. One of his priorities was to support the principle of equal access and to build an explicit commitment to equality in all aspects of the school's work.

The school's intake is socially and economically mixed but it has a higher than average proportion of pupils from moderately to severely disadvantaged backgrounds. A long-established local grammar school effectively creams the more middle class pupils in the area; indeed, in the current climate, which encourages parental choice and marketing strategies, the boast of some local primary schools is that they will 'get your child into the grammar school'. In the early 1980s a new comprehensive was built three miles away in an area characterised as 'aspiring working class' and Townley School lost an important dimension – a core of parents who were ambitious for their children. The school's profile changed again in 1990 when another local comprehensive, serving an area of extreme disadvantage, closed; Townley School took about half the pupils. The numbers are now buoyant – 1200 plus, with an 8 form entry – but the profile of disadvantage has intensified. A new threat in the 1990s is to the school's sixth form, which currently has 90 pupils, as plans for tertiary reorganisation are discussed in the borough.

The borough has a substantial black population but the community which Townley School now draws from is white working class. Indeed, the school is anxious that its current popularity may reflect local racism, with some white families opting to send their children here because it is seen as 'the all-white school'. The largest minority group are the travelling children.

The pupils

'It's a decent school, that, a decent school' said the taxi driver on my first visit. Although there is violence within the community, which often involves young women as well as young men, pupils' behaviour in school is generally thought to be reasonable. The main problem is settling pupils down at the beginning of the 70 minute lessons, and sustaining their attention during the final ten minutes.

The pupils are described by different staff as 'biddable', 'straight', 'friendly', 'fairly talkative and outspoken'. A new teacher comments:

Pupils are noisier and the pupils are a lot more forthright than at my previous school, you know. They will say what they're thinking without the intention, I would say, of being rude or insolent. I mean their first comment might be, 'You've had your hair cut, Miss' . . . They do seem to be older and more worldlywise, more streetwise . . . They're generally fairly friendly. And they like attention.

An established teacher offers her profile of the pupils:

They will stand up for themselves and want to express an opinion, want you to know how they feel. But outside the school gates I think the girls and boys are far less confident than they would have you believe.

Staff generally agree that the main problem is one of low expectations:

The children, without a teacher behind them, lack motivation. Most of them don't see the need to succeed. You obviously have the exceptions but they're a minority. And you have an attendance problem. You have an actual physical motivation problem in the classroom. You have a problem getting them to do homework or preparation work.

Attendance and non-attendance patterns are little different from the norm for inner city schools but they do, as in every similar school, make it difficult for teachers to ensure that pupils experience continuity and coherence in their learning. Although teachers acknowledge that pupils will 'vote with their feet' if they find particular lessons boring, some of the problems seem to lie in community habits, as a teacher explains:

There is truancy that is parentally connived: 'You stay at home and look after the baby' or 'The gas man is coming this afternoon and you stay at home and let him in'. But there's also the comment from the kid: 'Mum, I'm only doing this in this lesson so I won't bother going in, okay?' and mum says, 'Okay'.

With parents unambitious for their children, a work ethic is hard to build, even though pupils themselves say that they want to learn. A new programme of flexible learning is being planned but staff are wary: 'If you have unmotivated children, how can you get them to support their own learning?' asked one teacher.

The problem is compounded by some teachers who continue to judge pupils by their past performance and do not always recognise the significance of even small changes in the pattern of aspirations; they do not seem to believe, in any profound way, that society will allow these children to succeed and they are therefore sceptical of the very things which might help the children feel that they are 'born into possibilities'.

At the same time, the individual support that so many pupils need is draining of staff time and energy, which, in a less star-crossed setting, might go into plans for raising expectations and achievement levels. One tutor gives a thumbnail sketch of the members of his tutor group, now in their fifth year (year 11) of secondary school. These are the first few he talked about; they are fairly representative of the form as a whole, although among the remaining 16 were two pupils, one boy and one girl, who were experiencing very severe levels of distress. The first pupil on the register is a boy who has experimented with drugs, who smokes heavily and is under surveillance by a child guidance officer. The second is a boy who tries very hard with his work, whose parents want him to do well, but his grades, despite his efforts, are low. The third is a boy who is absent for stretches of time, usually helping his mother, who has had a nervous breakdown, look after four younger brothers and sisters: 'When he comes to school he's just tired'. Fourth is a girl who likes school – 'School is the most pleasant experience of her life: her father's been in prison, there's little furniture in the family home'. Fifth is a well cared for boy from a very strict background who is only comfortable in highly disciplined structures which do not require initiative. Then there is a very bright boy whose main problem is getting up in the morning; he is usually late for school. Then there is a girl from a travelling family which has now settled locally. Both her parents had recently got into trouble with the law; she spends a lot of time helping look after younger brothers and sisters. Next is a boy who lives with his mother and brothers and sisters and who does not attend regularly. Ninth is a girl from a middle class background who is able but whose self-esteem and aspirations are very low; as a result she is poorly motivated in relation to GCSE work.

Many of the school's pupils inhabit a small world: 'They don't move far, even to the big town just a few miles away'. The school tries to compensate by organising visits but many parents are not able to pay and, increasingly, the school can't afford to subsidise.

The development of the equal opportunities policy: the first three years

Townley School has had, and continues to have, a lot to contend with. It is not the easiest of contexts in which to develop an active whole-school policy on equal opportunity and equal access.

Before the present initiative started in 1988, the school had many of the characteristics of 'unreconstructed' traditional secondary schools. The senior management team were all male; the distribution of male and female teachers across departments and across posts of responsibility was predictably patriarchal. Pupils had been organised in three broad ability streams – the 'bottom' one known internally as 'the Q & S' (Queer and Strange stream). Nor had the school given much attention to the day-to-day experiences of its minority of travelling children.

On the whole, the senior management team and the equal opportunities committee have steered a course between the moral compulsion of 'causes and crusades' on the one hand and authoritarian diktat on the other. Their strategy has been to establish a simple policy, to communicate the policy widely among staff, among pupils and within the community, and to invoke it as a means of securing conformity of practice among staff and pupils. There is, still, a long-term aspiration that staff attitudes will change so that colleagues act from personal conviction and not just professional accountability, but, realistically, it is seen as enough at first if a policy can be arrived at which does command action, even though people feel differently about the significance of the principles that lie behind the policy. Neglect of the policy, once it is established, can be met by the challenge: 'This is the school policy; if you don't want to honour it in your practice then you may need to think whether this is the right place for you to teach'.

The decision to put equality issues on the agenda was not fuelled by any passionate sense of outrage within the staff of the school. It happened because an outsider, a new head, together with his deputy (the present head) took the first steps. Since 'equality' was in the air at the time, other teachers were able to voice their support. But development has been a struggle.

Harry is the present deputy head and responsibility for equal opportunities was built into his job specification. Before his appointment there had been some tentative planning for multi-cultural work but little had been done. Harry inherited a 'multi-cultural filing cabinet' – 'files for everything and lots of wonderful looking bits of paper, but I couldn't find any reality'. His priority was to translate vague ideas into action. There was already a working party on multi-cultural issues but 'it was very frightened of the topic and was pussyfooting around it'. Harry chose to merge it with the recently established Curriculum Awareness Group (CAG) and to open up the brief. He decided to highlight gender initially 'as a stalking horse' and to build up work on race and disability alongside it but at a slower pace.

He knew that creating a whole-school policy would not in practice be easy. There was little existing sense of a 'whole-school' spirit. At one time, for instance, the school had had eight different staff rooms and the habit of segregation into groups was exacerbated by the two very different cultures of the lower and upper schools which were on different sites. In such a 'dispersed centres' structure, the senior management team is unable to mix easily with the whole staff except on formal occasions, and habits die hard. Even now, with one main staffroom – there are still some 'minor' department-based social centres – the senior management team tends not to enter the staffroom except on 'business'.

Harry and his colleagues on CAG, decided to relaunch the equal opportunities issue with something of a splash – an after-school meeting with wine and cheese and some activities which were designed to 'ease' colleagues into the serious issues. All staff were invited. There were personalised invitations and regular, slightly zany notices in the school bulletin: 'EO's coming' (echoing the 'ET' film publicity). Harry was pleased with the 60 per cent staff attendance. Such a gathering was itself a breakthrough in the school. After some ice-breaking exercises (necessary in a staff of over 100) Harry and members of CAG presented a role play featuring a sexist male teacher in the classroom. They played for laughs. This episode was followed by a group activity – the groups had been carefully constructed in advance – and the task was to design a non-equal-opportunities school. The constructions included the following details: 'Office ladies, dinner ladies, male caretakers, male technicians, female cleaners and a groundsman'; 'The responsibilities of the senior mistress: girls' welfare; charity events; looking after visitors, tea for the governors'; profile of a head of Upper School: 'Male, 35 years old and a high flyer'; profile of a head of Lower School: 'Female and nearly 60'. Predictably, some details struck home and people present acknowledged that their own school was in some respects much like the one they had constructed.

Harry's concern now was to capitalise on the new sense of concerted attention. Different topics were identified for enquiry and small teams were formed: they worked on teaching materials, teacher expectations, values and prejudices, peer pressure, examination results. The activities started well: 'More and more people came to discuss – it was really bubbly for a while' (Harry) but it was difficult to sustain the momentum given the new waves of pressure now coming in from outside the school – in particular from the demands of implementing the national curriculum. Some working groups collapsed but the reports of those that completed their tasks were circulated to all staff, and the findings of the prejudice group, in particular, generated considerable concern. An attitude enquiry had been used to find out how pupils felt about various potential 'neighbours'. It emerged that 'the least favourite group' were the travellers whose children were in fact the largest minority group in the school. Local solidarity, traditional morality, and the prevailing sexism of the area were also reflected in the responses, and considerable numbers of pupils listed 'unmarried parents', 'unmarried mothers', and 'Northerners' as people they did not want to interact with.

The next event planned by Harry and CAG was a two-day conference held off-site at a hotel; attendance was required. The conference included sessions on the hearing impaired, the physically handicapped, being blind, travellers, and the health of women in the locality. A teacher from another school described her experience of developing an EO policy, and teachers from Townley School talked about equal opportunities development work in their subjects. There was a session called 'What about the boys?', a session by a black teacher on equal opportunities policy in his school, and a session from a national bank called 'Equal opportunities policy in action'.

After the event a four-side evaluation sheet was circulated to all staff. The tone and content signalled that equal opportunities was being taken seriously. Staff non-attenders or partial attenders (only two) were named, and reasons were given in the evaluation sheet for their absence. Staff were also reminded that the conference had several aims: to bring in experience from outside the usual educational network; to stimulate and motivate and to be controversial; to provide opportunities to learn from each other's experiences; and to create a climate for personal challenge and reflection. The summary of evaluative comments was a clear indication of the different starting points within the staff as a whole and the difficulty of moving quickly towards an agreed and supported position on equal opportunities. For instance, some staff felt that the conference was well-judged and well-balanced. A minority of respondents said that it was too 'political' (indeed, some defensively critical comments centred on the challenging eloquence of the black keynote speaker). Some questioned the relevance of the conference, asking why they needed to bother with equal opportunities, and quite a lot of staff, challenged by the input, thought that the only problem was lack of time to pursue the issues in depth.

Harry had been under no illusions. Progress was not going to be easy. As equal opportunities 'action man' he had to face both the accusations of the minority who were committed to equal opportunities and who felt that more should be done, and quickly, and the less publicly vociferous minority who resented the school's decision to take equal opportunities policy and practice seriously. It is not easy for the person in the middle to maintain commitment and a sense of direction – but he did. However, as he later said, 'It was one of the worst periods of my life . . . there was a lot of bitchiness and I felt that it was all slipping away from me'. But with the support of the head and the senior management team, he kept going.

Two events in particular signalled to staff that things were going to change. First, was the reordering of registers – a suggestion made at the wine and cheese evening and picked up by the head for immediate action. The move was greeted with vehemence by some staff, including accusations that not organising the registers alphabetically by boys and then girls was 'against the law'. Second, following the increase in pupil numbers, two new deputy head appointments were advertised. The head and the one male deputy knew that the governors were not sympathetic to the idea of positive discrimination in favour of women and were determined to appoint the two best candidates, whether male or female. Five candidates were shortlisted, three men and two women. In the event, the two women were appointed. The deputy head recalls the reaction in the staffroom:

When the head announced it there was an argument in the staffroom with the men saying 'It's unfair. It's affected our careers. It's not on, people messing us around. How can they justify it?' Big argument. A Spaniard who was teaching here then said: 'What are people arguing about, please? Why?' It was explained to him and he walked out [in disgust at the men's responses]. Then a woman got up and said, 'Do you realise that if it had been two men (appointed) you wouldn't be arguing at all? You wouldn't be saying anything'. And she walked out. So that was the state of play in the staffroom.

In fact, Harry decided to enhance the formal profile of equal opportunities and, with the head's support, an Equal Opportunities Committee was established, replacing the old Curriculum Awareness Group. An EO coordinator was appointed on an A allowance but the fact that the appointment was for two years only was criticised by some staff who felt that a short-term appointment smacked of tokenism – an interpretation denied by the senior management team on the grounds that, once a policy and programme of work was in place, it was all too easy for staff to sit back and think, 'Oh, we can leave that to the equal opportunities person'. At the same time, an allowance was also given for a programme of work with the school's travelling children. Some inservice days were allowed for each department to initiate development work on equal opportunities, including a review of teaching materials. A termly in-school equal opportunities publication was launched in line with 'the management policy of constant publicity to maintain equal opportunities at the forefront of staff awareness' (Harry), and a continuing series of whole-school events was planned and implemented.

During the new Committee's first year of activity, equal opportunities policy documents were drafted, discussed and redrafted. Speakers from outside were brought into school at intervals as a deliberate part of the policy of sustaining awareness. Each department was also obliged to draw up its own development plan. Although the focus had been mainly on gender, issues of ethnicity and disability had not been neglected: for instance, money was reserved to ensure that senior members of all departments attended a race awareness training course, and appropriate LEA officers were brought in to give help and advice to staff about the needs of the school's small but increasing number of physically disabled pupils.

During this period, Harry, the deputy, made it his responsibility to gather, analyse and circulate hard data from which to begin to view gender issues in each curriculum area; he focused mainly on option choices and examination entries and results. He also invited staff cooperation in keeping a full and accurate record of any reported behavioural incidents that appeared to have a sexist or racist dimension.

By the autumn of 1991, three years after the informal start to the work, Harry had succeeded in putting in place 'a working policy and not just a paper policy'. Different versions were prepared for staff, for pupils and for parents. Common to all three versions was the statement: 'Equal Opportunities at Townley School means care, respect, consideration and courtesy from all, for all and to all'. The document for pupils emphasised fairness, justice and security:

Everyone at Townley School must feel secure and know that the school will not accept any form of unfair discrimination or prejudiced behaviour. Pupils should report any incident of spoken or physical bullying to a member of staff who will take immediate action.

The document for staff makes it clear that all colleagues 'are expected to implement policy guidelines and use them with consistency'. It helpfully includes numerous examples of the sort of incident that is deemed unacceptable, as well as a range of possible responses to such incidents. There is a strong restatement of the principle that all manifestations of violence or abuse, whether spoken or physical, 'must be challenged by authority in a constant attempt to eradicate it'. The document goes on to list some examples of name calling: the list, although far from comprehensive, is sufficient to remind staff that even those terms which are fairly familiar are nonetheless unacceptable.

The policy documents were distributed among parents and pupils and staff, and displayed on walls and corridors. The circulation to parents was important because, in particular, it allowed staff to make reference to the document when writing home to report particular incidents that contravened the policy.

The policy statements are simple and plain-spoken and they reflect the school's statement about rules: 'There are few rules but one over-riding principle: to show care and courtesy to all in the school'. Some gendered practices continue which are defended by the departments concerned (see later) although they may increasingly be subject to critical comment by pupils.

A lot had been achieved when, in 1990–91, the special allowance for the EO coordinator, Helena, came to an end but there was still a long way to go. Her realism had stood her in good stead during her two years of hard work and she said, looking back: 'I went into that position knowing that I wasn't going to change everybody's attitude'. The hope was that the Equal Opportunities Committee would continue with a volunteer chair; in fact, there were no volunteers and Harry agreed not only to take over the chairing but also, with Helena's help, to deal with the increasing amount of paper work as more items of 'hard evidence' were collected and circulated to staff.

Sustaining the momentum

The cajoling and encouraging had, by now, a new sharpness. The senior management team (SMT) continued to take the equal oppor-tunities issue very seriously indeed. It was not, as some had hoped, just the management team's 'flavour of the month'. It was announced that 'the promotion of equal opportunities now constitutes a major responsibility incorporated into the line management roles' and SMT initiated a regular review meeting with departmental teams and equal opportunities was on the agenda for each meeting. The team also extended Harry's work on the collection, analysis and presentation, from a gender perspective, of relevant data that would feed departmental discussions. The data showed that predictable patterns were still apparent in some areas – textiles, biology, CDT, dance – and these areas were then targeted for special action and surveillance. Personal, Social and Health Education (PSHE) was redesigned to carry a stronger equal opportunities component. Referral slips – used when pupils' behaviour is formally reported and recorded – were modified so that teachers could comment on any incident that appeared to have a sexist or racist dimension. Any evidence of sexist or racist abuse was met with a written statement to parents saying that such behaviour contravened the school's policy.

Of course, as the senior management team knew, things don't always go smoothly. The school is large and at the time of the fieldwork there were other developments that were requiring urgent attention: plans to bring the lower and upper school onto the same site; the building of a new drama complex and swimming pool; the design and introduction of a set of varied 'food bars' for the school and its attached community centre. Staff were also undertaking inservice activities relating to the Education Reform Act and Harry noted: 'Juggling of priorities is difficult because for the average trooper in the classroom, the national curriculum, coping with kids, the moves are all more immediately pressing'.

Importantly, small setbacks did not blunt the determination. An encouraging note was that, despite all the competing pressures, staff had identified a number of areas where they felt attention should now be focused: enhancing students' general awareness (by organising, for instance, an Equal Opportunities Day); increasing girls' awareness of post-school opportunities; overcoming the girls'/boys' subject barrier in options; more on the needs of the left-handed; introducing work on homosexuality; looking at discrimination and age – particularly in relation to staff responsibilities; and more on disability and physical access within the school. It was also suggested that more should be done to help with the change of attitudes and practices among support staff, including caretakers, cleaners, meals supervisors and technicians.

Building a working commitment across the staff

Perhaps the greatest challenge in any large school is to bring a collection of individuals and departments to some sense of unity about principles and practices. The task is even more difficult when it engages values that are likely to conflict with personal life styles and subject-based traditions. The nature of whole-school change is, as yet, not well understood and the problems should not be under-estimated. Nor should the achievements. It is not just a question of recognising a group of advocates and a group of adversaries; such broad labels in fact conceal a range of positions and personal/professional tensions. It is important to understand what this means in terms of establishing a school policy that actually guides practice right through the school.

In Townley School the group of more or less 'committed' staff is, interestingly, far from uniform in the nature of their personal experiences of equal opportunities. There are women who were brought up in all-female households and/or who went to all-girls schools and who have felt 'naturally' competent over a range of tasks and free to be aspiring in their own lives and careers. They want female pupils in the school to have the same sense of possibility. There are women whose commitment to equality stems more from the struggles and frustrations that they have experienced in their working lives or in their early years of schooling. For instance, one teacher recalls the origin of her own commitment:

I think I actually started becoming a feminist when I was seven. Looking back on when they were picking boys out of my class at school to be altar boys, I was actually incensed that I couldn't be chosen – not because I was particularly religious but simply because it was seen as an honour, as being special, as being something that people would praise you for . . . I didn't like the way that things were assumed about my role in society and what young ladies should and shouldn't do and all that sort of thing.

There are also women who have compartmentalised their commitment: at home they fulfil the traditional expectations of a woman's role while at school they actively support equality issues.

There are men whose perceptions have been changed through the experience of their female partners: 'I'm married to a woman who is very keenly aware of equal opportunities and very interested in it herself so it's obviously at the forefront of conversation'. And there are men who describe themselves, for whatever reason, as 'recently liberated' and who are still unravelling the nature of their own commitment and the contradictions that they find in their own behaviour: what is important is that they are now recognising the dissonance and acknowledging it.

What is unusual about this school is that there is no small, clearly defined group of women, or women and men, who are unified through a passionately outspoken concern for equality issues; there is no group that can be labelled 'the feminists', no group that people can react against as 'the extremists'. Equally, it is not easy to identify a clear group of adversaries. They exist at some level but they no longer own their opposition publicly. As one teacher said, 'colleagues are very careful about hiding their attitudes'. I interviewed some who were personally uncommitted, and their stories were about the pull of other priorities or the strength of the conventions within their discipline which are seen to provide some kind of legitimation for dealing differently with boys and girls – even though the pupils themselves may be unhappy with these conventions. The fieldwork suggested that the positions of the majority of staff were subtly fanned out between the extremes of 'adversary' and 'advocate'.

Among those who would want to claim that they are 'pro EO' there are teachers who seem genuinely to think that equalising opportunity is a simple matter; they say, 'We treat them as students or clients . . . It's irrelevant whether they're boys or girls' and 'The opportunities are there for them if they wish to grasp them' – as though the provision of opportunities is enough, as though the school's structures are intrinsically free from bias, and as though the social pressure on young people to conform to stereotypes does not exist. Standing alongside this group are the 'easy riders' who say – perhaps as a way of conserving energy – that 'if the national curriculum is done in a reasonable manner, then the race and gender things should follow': in short, there's no need to make any special effort. There are also those whose support extends as far as meeting the minimum requirements: 'I draw the pupils' attention to it (the school policy) and basically I present them with the facts . . . whether they participate is up to them'.

Then there are those who claim to be in sympathy but who do not support collective action. Some argue that equal opportunities, by definition, means that everyone is free to act according to their principles: 'There are people who don't agree with it across the school – that's fair enough; they're entitled to their own view'; or: 'There are one or two with more traditional views but I don't think that influences their teaching'.

Then there are those who see equal opportunities as an extension of the humanitarian principles that guide their own action; for them, equality is a profoundly personal commitment and they may, unless they have a strong sense of public mission, distance themselves from the urgent activity of constructing a whole-school code of conduct. Indeed, the strength of their own conviction can make them resentful of the school's attempts to monitor their practice: 'I believe myself to be as fair and equitable to everybody as I possibly can and I tend to resent people telling me to do things different and reminding me that "This is the school's policy" '.

There are teachers who are supportive but pessimistic: 'You can raise their (the pupils') awareness but there comes a point where you know . . . you're going to have a limited effect'. Such pessimism can, of course, inhibit positive action and blunt perception; indeed, some people persist in claiming that the 'vision of life' of female pupils in the school is that 'they will become a wife and mother and will never have to work'. This is a view of young women which both denies the struggles over identity and futures that many of them are experiencing and discounts the responsibility carried by local women whose wages may be supporting an unemployed partner as well as sons and daughters. A variant of the pessimistic position is the view that it is difficult to convert the local community and that equal opportunities therefore encourages young people to have 'false expectations'.

Then there are those who are personally committed but who have senior colleagues in their department who have set different priorities – equal opportunities is seen as 'just another pressure' and for all members of the department preparing pupils for the examinations 'has to take precedence over everything'.

And finally there are teachers, both men and women, who are actively committed and whose commitment reflects an urgent concern that the school should be doing more for young people, and for young women in particular.

The goal for the senior management team, in the face of such a range of positions, is to arrive at some sort of working consensus that will keep the majority of staff moving forward. The group of 'out and out antis' is 'now very small': there are still a few women, it seems, who 'think it a complete and utter waste of time' and some men who are resentful that colleagues assume that it will be men who are in opposition. But no-one seems to think that the 'antis', whatever their reasons, represent a sufficiently critical mass to impede progress: 'As it's gone on, and because so many staff have been involved, it's become part of the institution. It's part of Townley School now. So we're on the upward path of change'. But the pressure, and the sense of purposeful development, still need to be maintained.

In all institutional settings where changes of this kind are being pursued there will be a struggle. But as teachers internalise the new values, so the capacity of any minority of 'antis' to sustain different practices in the privacy of their own classrooms becomes increasingly difficult. Pupils realise that such behaviour is at odds with the school's new habits and will often learn to say so. Over time, the simultaneous pressure from policy and from pupils can ensure at least a minimal commitment to the letter of the school's equality 'law' – and conforming may, over time, modify the individual's personal value system.

Building a working commitment across departments

Even as there are different shades of commitment among teachers, so there are differences between departments which go beyond the sum of the commitments of individual members of those departments. Departments differ in the strength of their conventions for sustaining gendered images and practices. Individual commitments come into play in relation to the readiness to accept or challenge these conventions.

In the space of its three-year plan, Townley School's Equal Opportunities Committee set out to initiate review and development on three different curriculum fronts: teaching materials; teaching content and tasks; and classroom interaction. Departmental representatives were responsible for activating work with their colleagues and progress was monitored. An early move was the requirement that all departments produce their own equal opportunities statement, following departmental discussion, together with an action plan which indicated priorities for development. Even though, at worst, the commitment to the plan is less strong within some departments than others, nonetheless all members of staff have participated in the exercise, the statements and plans have been circulated to all staff, and they will form the basis of monitoring discussions between departments and members of the senior management team.

Within the statements and plans there were a few qualifying phrases that might indicate some diffidence or scepticism. For example, two departments claimed that they would 'actively facilitate the equal participation of all students' but added the phrase 'whenever possible'. Another department promised to take action on all sexist or racist incidents that occurred during lessons but added: 'incidents may be deferred to the end of the lesson'. Overall, the sense of shared purpose and consistency of practice that the exercise engendered was impressive.

The Special Needs Department had a five-point action plan:

1 To develop a more positive image of travellers.
2 To monitor the progress of bilingual pupils.

3 To review the balance of sexes in withdrawal groups (which are mainly boys) and to see whether the low-achieving female pupils are being given enough attention and support.
4 To develop work on identifying and supporting pupils with hearing difficulties.
5 To discuss with the LEA's Mobility Officer changes needed in and around the school site to help the visually handicapped.

The CDT Department (which now has one female part-time technology teacher) offered the following statement and plan:

The CDT department recognises that the nature of CDT and its associated image and attitudes require special attention being paid to some aspects of presentation and teaching techniques. The department is committed to:

1 Schemes of work, literature and projects appropriate to all pupils.
2 Equal access to the subject for all pupils.
3 Providing a working environment in which all pupils feel comfortable.
4 Giving extra support to pupils whose background has limited their prior experience of aspects of CDT.
5 Emphasising career opportunities for all pupils based on experiences in CDT.
6 Recognising that some groups of pupils can monopolise equipment and staff, and to compensate for this as necessary.

The complexity of the task of change differs, of course, from subject area to subject area and is influenced both by the strength, nationally, of gendered images of the subject and by the strength, locally, of particular departmental conventions. There are areas of the curriculum which have, like CDT, traditionally presented problems for equal opportunities. But what about mathematics? In terms of staffing, the department has equal numbers of men and women although the promoted posts are held by full-time and longer serving male teachers. The commitment to equal opportunities is not equally strong for all members. Nevertheless, progress has been made. Maths is one of two subjects in the school which bands pupils (the other is modern languages) and in each year there is one top set, the other sets being equal. At the time of the fieldwork the girls in the top set in year 10 outnumbered the boys by two-to-one and were performing better. Departmental concern highlighted the danger of 'turning the lads off if you start going on and on about the girls' – which, it seems, is how equal opportunities is sometimes perceived. The department has, however, constructed a short unit on the history of the subject which shows that women have made a significant contribution to the development of mathematical knowledge.

Perhaps the most contentious curriculum area is the PE/games/dance component of the school's expressive arts curriculum. The challenge of equal access has been heard and the possibilities of change were being examined, although somewhat warily, by the staff. Some claim, with some justice, that particular problems are created in PE by gendered models of participation and practice that are nationally accepted. At the time of the fieldwork, the curriculum included single-sex PE for pupils in years 7, 8 and 9 and mixed PE for pupils in years 10 and 11. Within the mixed groups there are options and the claim is that: 'They select their own, (and) there is no bias' – other, of course, than the habits and choices that the pupils have been socialised into making. Data on option choices must now be kept and circulated and it is clear that football remains an exclusively male option. Football is problematic: because it is not part of the girls' curriculum in years 7 to 9 girls do not acquire the skills that would allow them to play equally alongside boys in years 10 and 11. However, if they wish, girls may form their own team. A teacher confirms the department's readiness to mirror society's habits with the argument of biological difference: 'Men do tend to be stronger than females and so it wouldn't be much of a game to put them against each other'. In school, it is argued, there are the complicating factors of changing room surveillance, showers, timetabling and the traditional skills biases of the male and female staff. Some justification is offered through the theoretical notion that in fact it does not matter whether they play football or hockey since both boys and girls are having experience of the skills and logics of 'invasion games'. The problem is, of course, that pupils do not see it that way! To meddle with football is seen as dangerous because it is the lynchpin of the male culture of the region. It is easier for staff to contemplate mixed cricket which appears not to have quite such a cult following locally.

Colleagues who challenge the departmental approach are told: 'You know, we only keep boys and girls separate for specific reasons . . . There's more to it than just what immediately meets the eye'. Dance has in fact been mixed for four years and there are male as well as female dance teachers. There is some fear among staff that standards may not be as high as they were in the old 'girls only' classes and the perception of the 'different' strengths of the male and female students conforms to traditional stereotypical patterns: 'The girls may be more thoughtful about pointing their toes and getting their legs together but the lads perhaps introduce greater ideas, you know, imagination'. It was notable that in the curriculum review the PE department merely listed the different activities that they offered in each year under the headings 'boys' and 'girls'.

It is clear that not all members of the PE department are in agreement about current policy: but 'Staff attitude is changing' and several of the more gendered conventions are likely to come 'under review'. However, the department is responding well to the integration of physically disabled pupils – pupils who are partially sighted or who are in wheelchairs. Expert advice is offered by a local PE adviser with special experience of special needs and a lot of support is offered by other pupils. Posters have been put in the changing room celebrating the achievements in sport of the physically disabled.

The advances in thinking and planning generated by the curriculum review were, in many curriculum areas, encouraging; in others, staff were, at the very least, challenged to defend their practices publicly and even in the more reluctant departments there was evidence of some rethinking. Pressure was sustained by the curriculum 'audit' which was launched a year later and each department was asked to explain (in relation to three terms of work for years 7, 8 and 9 – i.e., 9 entries in all) what the main content would be and how the concern with equal opportunities would be reflected. The responses showed, overall, a readiness now to take on multi-ethnic dimensions as well as gender dimensions and there were also some departments where it was seen as relevant to tackle issues of sexuality and issues of bullying and harassment. Here are some examples (undifferentiated by term and year):

Drama   Sex roles at home; handling bullying at school; role reversals in industrial relations.

Art   Looking at and representing male and female figures.

English Sexism, racism and ageism in a range of texts; male and female choices in newspapers and magazines.

CDT   The design and manufacture of objects that have, in themselves, no obvious male/gender associations – such as identity fobs, letter racks, coat hooks, finger rings, etc.

Music   Awareness and appreciation of non-European musical cultures; women in pop.

Dance }
Drama } Heroes and heroines – challenging stereotypes.

History Women's rights.

The majority of departments responded positively.

Relationships

Teacher-teacher relationships

The concern with equality issues affects not only the way teachers interact with pupils and the way that pupils interact with each other, but also the way that staff interact with each other. The EO document for staff includes a sentence on appointments. It promises 'an equal opportunities policy for the recruitment, selection and promotion of staff' and 'equal access to personal and professional development courses'. But it mainly focuses on staff room interaction. Some advice is offered about handling particular comments or behaviours:

Do not act aggressively or allow the incident to be trivialised; if it offends explain carefully and calmly why the joke/comment/behaviour is offensive to you; discuss the wider issues with the colleague concerned; when in doubt seek advice/support from a senior colleague in whom you feel confident. Do not ignore the situation.

But staff room situations are in fact fairly complex. An experienced teacher, who acknowledges her own ambivalence towards the school's equal opportunities policy, comments: 'The railing (that goes on) in the staff room from the blokes to the women is fine if you can take it, and I think it is a pity if we lose it all, but I am aware that it is offensive to some people and, no, I don't think they should have to put up with it'. Another senior woman, a strong supporter of the EO policy, explained that she had learned to use patient good humour in the face of male colleagues who seemed only able to cope with her seniority through an essentially good natured mockery. Jokes are, of course, an important part of the staff room culture; they signal a respite from the company of adolescents – a withdrawal into an adult world – and they offer some release, through the sense of being in relaxed and cooperative company – from the tensions and pressures that staff bring from the classroom. Nonetheless, a footnote in the EO document for staff warns: 'Sexist, racist or insensitive jokes or comments amongst staff, directed towards colleagues, pupils or parents, are harmful. They destroy relationships and hinder the development of a good working environment'. Ironically, to some extent, these jokes, tolerated by the majority, have in fact served as the anchor of the 'good working environment'. Once the content of the staff room exchanges comes under scrutiny – and the policy statement is uncompromising here – then a temporary vacuum may be created which, at a time of pressure, could be dysfunctional. A new culture takes time to grow. Staff are coping with this by allowing some residual licence on the gender front; the racist joke, however, is now likely to be met by 'a stunned silence'. The transitional culture allows the sexually-toned exchanges provided that the exponents are honest about acknowledging their 'lapses'.

Interestingly, a similar dilemma has been experienced by some teachers in relation to dealing with sexist language among pupils. One said:

How do you explain to them that the saying, 'he's a girl' as a form of insult is awful? How do you actually do that without deadening the conversation? They may never speak to you again, sounding off as if you're a stuffed shirt moralist. It's very difficult and a very sensitive thing to be able to say, 'I really don't feel that that's an acceptable thing to say'. You can hit the mark, but more often than not you won't. You won't get through. It's difficult.

This teacher was anxious about the importance of maintaining good relationships with pupils in a school where it is crucial that each child feels that there is someone on the staff whom she or he can talk to easily. There are a number of issues to do with the language of social exchange, the language of trust, and the language of reprimand which schools may need to reflect on.

Teacher–pupil relationships
Teacher–pupil interaction in the classroom is perhaps the most difficult aspect of equality for a school to monitor in any systematic way. Teacher–teacher observation partnerships can be helpful but they tend to require additional staffing and this, at present, would be beyond the scope of a school which often has a longish day-to-day cover list and little money to support professional development outside its already agreed priorities. The pupils themselves are aware of gender bias in the classroom and seem increasingly ready to comment, although many have yet to learn how criticism can be offered in a constructive rather than triumphant or vindictive way.

There was evidence that pupils understood what counts as poor equal opportunities practice: 'It's wrong whenever a man teacher sends the boys out first and a woman teacher sends the girls out first' (year 9); or, 'Some teachers always say, "Boys wait and the ladies can go out first"' (year 10); or, 'Like when they need projectors carrying, it's always boys that they ask' (year 9); or, 'If it was a male teacher and if he taught the boys better like, more than the girls' (year 9); or, 'The girls can talk in class and the boys can't' (year 9).

Pupils were often mature in understanding the difficulty that they have in 'seeing' what has become familiar through habit; for instance, as one (year 9) said, 'I suppose there's a lot of things really but we're used to them. We've always done them; we wouldn't notice them'. And another pupil, this time in year 10, was beginning to understand the personal dilemmas that some of the teachers were confronting: 'I don't think some believe in it totally, but they do it'.

Interestingly, a few pupils commented critically on their own progress which they saw as an outcome of teacher-pupil relationships but not necessarily related to gender bias. They were beginning to sense that they could work harder, do better, but they had – as yet – no way of analysing the nature of the problem and instead offered a generalised and somewhat inarticulate blame. This snatch of dialogue was typical of the comments made by those pupils (year 10) who wanted to talk about learning:

JR: So you'd like it to be a bit stricter?
P1: Yeah, so we could learn somat.
P2: You come to work, don't you?
P1: We learn enough but we could learn more.
JR: And why don't you learn more?
P1: Because of the teachers. If you don't want to do something, you don't bother. You just sit there. I reckon we should start and make 9 o'clock till 5 o'clock in the night.

Pupil-pupil relationships

Pupil-pupil relationships are in some respects more liberated than they were and also, in other respects, still caught in convention.

The school has a very small number of physically disabled pupils. Steve's disability was marked by his use of a wheelchair and his difficulty in speaking. But pupils were supportive of Steve to the point of protectiveness. An older pupil explained:

All the children in his year are quite friendly with him and they all like him and he's got like a few close friends ... His speech is, like, distorted but his friends have learned how to speak to him so if he's talking to anyone they'll be able to, like, translate.

Comments from teachers and from Steve's peers confirmed this view. The disabled do not threaten others; they do not form gangs; they are cared for and pupils are concerned that the school should improve physical access all round the site for pupils, like Steve, who are in wheelchairs.

Reactions to the school's travelling children are, however, very different. Because of the discontinuities in their learning, some find themselves placed in a class with pupils who are younger and to whom they seem bigger and – in a context where 'being older than the year below you' is a feature of the dominance patterns – they can seem potentially threatening. An older pupil who lives in the same area as many of the now temporarily housed travelling children and who has 'got used to them', gives a fairly balanced account of the typical pattern of perception and interaction:

Travelling kids generally seem to give us a tough time . . . You never see any of them in the sixth form. A lot of them don't stay on to do their exams . . . They don't think they can get into trouble at school because they can just move on . . . They give you a tough time and you aren't going to stand there and say, 'Oh well, I'll take it because, like, he's different from us', are you? You're going to give them a bit of aggro back . . . If they're nasty to you, you want to get them back . . . The school's just got an award for work with travellers . . . They don't give me a tough time because I live by them.

The survey conducted by the Equal Opportunities Committee indicated that the travellers were the object of considerable fear and distrust and, for their part, they afforded themselves some status and protection by moving around in groups – which are perceived as gangs. I was not able to learn what being at school was like for the travelling children themselves.

Some other year 12 pupils also talked about relationships between travelling children and others:

P1: Most of the time they're quite rough.
P2: They're always swearing and shouting at people.
P1: Some people would feel inclined to cause them physical harm but it's best to get it sorted out through legal (sic) channels.
P2: Some people are too frightened to say anything . . . being bullied and that.

I spoke with two of the school's few black pupils. One, a boy in year 9, had clearly experienced prejudice but was reluctant to talk about it. A young black woman in year 12 looked back on her early experiences and described her coping strategy:

I did used to [get called names] at first but now I don't. Nobody says anything any more. Like when you used to walk home you'd get people saying things . . . When you just walk off and ignore them that's when they don't like it because you show them you're not bothered. They don't like it when you ignore it.

A fellow pupil commented: 'I see them as being childish, criticising people because they're different races'. At the same time, the senior management team's records indicate that there is a racist dimension to many of the reported incidents involving the minority of black pupils – whether as acknowledged victims or as perceived aggressors. Disappointingly, the survey of year 11 pupils showed that just over 50 per cent felt that minor examples of threat to black pupils need not be reported to teachers, especially if the incidents occurred off the school premises.

Among the pupils that I interviewed in years 9, 10 and 12, many, as we have seen above, spoke in ways that indicated that they were very aware of equality issues as they related particularly to gender. A few pupils among the 30 that I spoke to remained 'unreconstructed' but not staunchly so and some, like Ross (year 10) were ready to acknowledge their own prejudices:

When I was in the third year (year 9) I used to do textiles and Miss says I am good at it but I said, 'Miss, I think it is a girls' subject' and Miss said, 'No. There are loads of men designers in clothes and that'. I said I thought it was a girls' subject and the teacher put me straight.

It was interesting to identify some of the finer nuances of change. For instance, one boy talked openly about winning the discus competition last year but this year being beaten by a girl; another boy explained that in lessons involving group work you tend to find boys' groups and girls' groups because 'I mean, you want to be with your best friends and they tend to be lads'. There were girls who explained that girls generally 'are being more boisterous now . . . I think it evolved because the girls want to find out what the lads went through' (year 10), and there was a girl who explained that boys 'treat us more like an equal now, more like one of their mates – not, "she's a girl; we'll not talk to her". A lot of them tend to come up and treat you like one of their best friends, like one of a gang, but some of them don't' (year 10). She described the behaviour of 'the ones that don't': 'If you are walking down a street with them and they see one of their friends that they hang about with, they will walk behind'.

The complexities of adolescent sexuality and dating behaviours tend, however, to reinstate some of the more conventional patterns. A year 10 girl explains: 'If you are going out with them, they show you off to their mates as if you're their object'. And some girls are, as yet, slightly uncertain what to do about conventional name calling:

P1: And boys call you a slag, a right bitch.
JR: And what do you do?
P1: Just turn away. Don't know what to say.
P2: We can't stop it.
P3: It's like a habit.

In this area, while name calling across the sexes seems to be largely a male habit, girls are more ready than in some other areas of the country to fight each other – not just on a one-to-one basis (usually about boyfriends) – but also, out of school, to beat up other girls in all-girl gangs. At the same time, there is some positive sense of girls needing to organise in order to stand up for themselves: 'We think we've got to fight to get our right or the boys are going to take over again' (year 10).

What we see then, in pupil-pupil relationships, is a varying kaleidoscope of feelings, concerns and aspirations as equality awareness develops and is either accommodated or wins through. Sometimes, equal opportunities may be 'used' as a justification for behaviours which are probably not expressive of any real commitment, but on the whole, there are many indications of change. It may be important that the tension between conventionally imaged roles in sexual relationships and the more openly defined roles that the school's equality programme outlines are explored with pupils in discussion.

A sense of progress

What progress has the school made? This is never a straightforward question to answer – for many reasons. As teachers at Townley School and at other schools, have come to realise, fundamental change – change that affects the deep structures of thinking and practice – is slow. Moreover, it is not easy for insiders to 'see' change that is gradual unless they consciously look back and recall how things were at a time when the school made its mark on their mind – the bench mark of, say, the first impressions registered by the teacher who came new to the school five or six years ago. Several teachers were able to comment from such a perspective. For instance, a female member of staff sees the concern with gender as part of a broader move to equal access: 'Before I came, equal opportunities wasn't a feature in the school at all'. Then, she recalls, there was a separate remedial department whereas now, as a matter of principle, children with learning needs are integrated. She recalled another feature: 'Some children were not given the chance to learn a second modern language because it was thought that "if they can't communicate in their own language, how can they cope with a new one?"'

Teachers who have very recently joined the school offer an important perspective. One teacher remarked how staff here make it clear that pupils must use a vocabulary of respect in talking about each other: name calling 'is stamped on very quickly'. Another teacher said that she was attracted to the post at Townley School because the job details gave such a strong message: 'It was unusual to find a school that made such a clear statement in information that was sent to candidates . . . and I don't think I was disappointed when I actually came'. She found that equality concerns were operating at many levels in the day-to-day work of the school. The school she left, 'although in some ways very progressive, was further behind Townley School in terms of developing a school policy for equal opportunities'. She was also struck by the fact that here 'senior management are very committed to it – the people in important places in the school are committed'. She went on, 'There are also people who just think the whole thing's a bit OTT [over the top] but even in the two terms I've been here I've felt that these people are now less noticeable'.

Another new female member of staff said that her move to the school 'was one of the best things I've ever done'. In her last school, the initiatives that she took as a woman she had no real recognition for and here she already feels a greater willingness to allow women ownership of the initiatives that they take: 'Here I feel I can speak my mind . . . sometimes, in the other school, you wanted to but you didn't . . . It's less threatening here for women'.

A recently appointed male colleague recalls his first impressions of the school:

I like the school. It's fair. It's got a sense of purpose, a sense of direction. There's things happening which are all moving in the right direction here . . .

It's got a thrust. It's got a sense of urgency about it and I think it's easy to pick that up when you walk into the school. The equal opps policy is up front, national curriculum is going forward at a steady and reasonable pace. It's all encouraging.

Established teachers who seek promotion and visit other schools for extended interviews also offered comparisons. 'I realised that we are a hell of a way down the road . . . I've been to schools where they've said they have an equal opportunities programme and they've knocked together a glossy package which is on the shelf, whereas we are actually putting our statements into practice'.

Similarly, older pupils (year 12) are able to look back and notice changes:

The school's come a long way because when we joined it, it was all male staff – like the heads, top jobs.

The school seems to encourage you to do subjects you enjoy. They don't say you shouldn't read this because you're a girl or you shouldn't do that, that's a boys' subject. If you enjoy it, why don't you do it anyway? That's their philosophy.

Some year 12 pupils recalled discriminatory practices in some subjects but thought that boys and girls are treated more equally now:

In the first year we did woodwork and metalwork and girls always seemed to get bad reports on that . . . The boys used to get bad reports in needlework . . . and they try to discourage you from doing it but by the time we got a bit further on they seemed to encourage you more. They don't say, 'You shouldn't read that because you're a girl' or, 'You shouldn't do that, that's a boys' subject'. If you enjoy it, why don't you do it anyway – that's the philosophy.

Some younger pupils (year 9) were also noting changes:

In CDT the other day he got two girls to take the machines instead of two lads. A lot of people put their hands up and he picked some girls.

Other younger pupils compared the present with a recent past that they had not experienced but had clearly been told about: 'In the old days, all the boys used to do CDT and all the girls used to do cooking . . .'. Older pupils (year 12), interestingly, made some comparisons between their parents' experience of schooling and their own experience in Townley School today:

My mum said when she was at school she had a maths teacher and they never taught the girls maths because he turned round and said, 'It's a waste of time teaching girls maths because they're only going to leave and get married and have kids anyway. You don't need maths to do that'.

At my mum's school it was an all-girls school anyway so they did everything but the only science they did was biology. They didn't do chemistry and they didn't do physics. But now, like here, you do everything.

A year 10 pupil compared his actual experience with his recent expectations:

In business systems you do typing to start off with and there were only two boys but we still like the subject. I thought it might be like a girls' subject because there were so many girls doing it but it's not.

Another year 10 boy compares his experience in the school that he moved from in another LEA:

Some of the teachers only paid attention to the boys – pulled all the girls right behind in class, so they had to have separate subjects so that they all got paid attention to. Here in lessons they do it equally.

Many of the pupils were themselves aware of what equality meant and older pupils were keen to debate the issues; their verdict on the school's progress with equal opportunities was: 'It's slowly changing'. What is interesting about the statements is the evidence they offer that pupils are observing, noting and reflecting on issues of equality.

What still needs to be done

Now that the frameworks that signal and sustain commitment are in place, what are the priorities for the future?

The overall concern must be simultaneously to strengthen existing perspectives and practices while still moving forward. Staff have already mentioned a number of possible areas that need to be brought within the frameworks or that need more focused attention. These include: teacher–pupil interaction in the classroom; monitoring of and support for ancillary staff (including meals supervisors); pupils' attitudes towards travelling children; enhancement of work on ethnicity. But the area that staff acknowledge to be the most difficult to tackle is that of pupils and their futures. The way that the school manages its advice about futures is pivotal. Ken is in charge of the careers advice and placement service. He works closely with Lara who is the school-based careers adviser. Lara is black and has a strong commitment to equality issues. Ken is a cheerful convert to equal opportunities and he has made many changes that reflect his new commitment: 'Kids can see us taking it seriously now'. He recalls how a few years back he would have noted a parent's opposition to a non-traditional career plan or placement and allowed himself to be influenced by it whereas he is now prepared to challenge a parent's position and talk things through.

He has totally redesigned the careers booklets which, before he began to 'see the light', offered starkly gendered images of jobs. As Ken said, 'I suddenly realised they were all blokes in the pictures'. On the work experience logs that Ken has recently introduced all pupils are required to think about equal opportunities issues. These are questions that they have to respond to:

1 Are some jobs mostly for males or females?
2 Which jobs and why do you think?
3 Describe the management organisation: are all the top people men?
4 Are males and females paid the same?
5 Are there facilities for the disabled?
6 Describe them and if there are none find out why not.

At 13 and 14 there is some evidence that more pupils are now beginning to think beyond the conventional; for instance, female pupils are saying things like, 'I'd like to be a fireman' or 'I want to be a painter and decorator'. However, when it comes to decisions about work experience, there is often loss of nerve and the analysis of placements for 1990/91 shows traditional patterns, although these patterns are beginning to fray at the edges in some occupational groups. In his annual report, Ken commented:

The picture is beginning to change, albeit slowly. This year two male students chose nursing, we had a female electrician and a female engineer, a female gardener, two female police. Hotel/catering, finance/accounts and computer work attracted roughly equal numbers.

Other occupational placements – nursery nursing, hairdressing and building craft, however, strongly reflected the strength of convention.

Ken has lived in the area most of his life and knows that the culture of the community is characterised by low aspiration and is one that 'sees things very clearly as men's jobs and women's jobs'. The 'low aspiration' that characterises the community in the eyes of Ken and other teachers also pulls pupils back towards predictable choices.

Ken and Lara are giving particular support to pupils who are under pressure, whether from family, peers or employers on work experience, to conform to the stereotypes. As Ken said, many of them 'could aim higher but they say, "Well, even if I do A levels, I still want to be a nursery nurse"'. The year 10 student (mentioned earlier) who said she wanted to be a painter and decorator commented on the struggle that being different would entail:

Student: I don't think I will get a job like that out in society but my uncle will probably give me a job because he runs his own business.
JR: Why don't you think you'll get one out in society?
Student: Because I'm a woman.

Lara, the careers officer attached to the school, talked about a female pupil, Carol, in year 11 who was facing difficult decisions about her future. While she wanted to do motor mechanics or engineering, she had deliberately put 'nursery nursing' on her work experience form and had persisted in that choice even though she had discussed her real ambitions, and her dilemmas, with Lara. Lara recalls the conversation:

Her father's a self-employed mechanic and she helps him fix cars. She can change radiators, she's knowledgeable about cars . . . She said that people laugh at her when they visit her father but she enjoys the work. She said she really wanted to become a motor mechanic and I said, 'Well, what about the nursery nursing?' and she replied, 'I'm not that keen on it but that's what I'm going to do'. So we talked about that and the peer pressure, the fact that her mother wanted her to do nursery nursing and her father didn't mind. . . . The outcome of the discussion is that she would like to speak to a female who does mechanics or engineering so we're going to arrange that when she comes back from work experience . . . Nobody knows that she wants to do motor mechanics – none of her friends know that she's interested . . . She's feeling now as if I've opened a can of worms and I think she's sort of wary rather than pleased and she's not sure whether she should go along this route or not.

Lara talked to Carol again after she had completed her work experience in the nursery:

Carol: I usually help my dad with fitting parts in cars. It was my first choice of a job for the future and since I wanted work experience I changed it because attitudes of people to a girl being a mechanic were sarcastic.
Lara: What sort of things were they saying?
Carol: Things like turning round and saying, 'It's not a job for a girl' and 'She's doing a boy's job' . . . People that my dad was doing cars for, they would turn round to me and say, 'I didn't expect a girl to be helping'. My mum didn't think it was a good idea. It makes me feel a bit sad because as I said I really want to do it and it is the way people react to you. They just put you off.

Another female pupil, Su, was also interested in engineering and had been placed for work experience in an appropriate firm where she had been up-front about her aspirations but had been obliged to work in the office:

Su: Well, I thought I might have problems with the men helping them with the machinery but in the office I thought I was going to do secretarial.
Lara: What sort of things were you given to do?
Su: Filing, photocopying, tea-urn. Just filing and filling out orders. They said, 'Everybody has to start at the bottom'. They were all boys you see. 'How could you get past the drawing board if you were pregnant?' 'How can you do a man's job with long fingernails?' They said I was good for making tea and little comments like that.
Lara: You call that 'little comments'? And how did that make you feel?
Su: I got used to them to be honest. I have got a friend that is going into engineering as well and she is really determined. I think she does very well.

Determination, as the following story also emphasises, is the significant factor. James, the director of the school's Community Centre, arranged for me to interview three young women in their twenties who had left school with good qualifications (O levels, A levels – and one had gone on to get a degree) and whose ambitions were blocked by the system. They all lived in Court Flats near the school and did some part-time work at the Community Centre. Support from the school and the strength they derived from their achievement in setting up and running a Residents' Association at the flats made them determined. All three are single parents (one is divorced) and none has an extended family in the locality. They feel strongly about their rights and want to escape from the poverty trap: they would like to work longer hours but cannot afford the child care costs; they would like to get out of the flats but can only get rehoused if they have more children – 'then you just become a mother and stay a mother and not a person'. One young woman had trained as a locksmith:

JR: So how did you get into that?
Jo: By being pushy. And I suppose being slightly different to the rest of the girls because they seemed to just take what came along at work. I mean I had to fight to get a female toilet. Well I think I started out on the right foot there. Luckily the company had a good union. But even while I was there I was paid a third less than my (male) colleagues for doing the same work. Then I was pregnant after signing a contract that I wouldn't have children.

Both Jill and Jane had experienced similar difficulties; Jill for instance, had worked in an organisation where 'women were looked at as the clerks and the men as management potential'. It was their work for the Residents' Association that kept them going: 'It makes you feel you're doing something, you're achieving something, you're getting somewhere, you're not just sitting at home'. Even here, though, they had a struggle in facing the range of reactions from male and female tenants and from the council members whom they had to approach in their capacity as Secretary, Treasurer and Chair of the Association: 'People thought we'd set up a "Toddlers' Group" not a "Residents' Association" '. At first, the men who attended the meetings regarded them, they thought, as 'a bit of skirt', but now they were taken seriously. 'It helps', said Jo 'that we're fairly articulate; we talk like men, I think – we don't beat about the bush'.

The irony, for an aware sixth former, is that however well the school is doing with equality issues, the world that she and her friends will soon move into full-time is a long way behind the school:

You've got equal opportunities in school and then you get out into work and they treat you like a bit of . . . You're a woman or you're black and I think the doors shut in your face.

There is an acknowledgement within the school that more attention needs to be given to the dilemmas that young women face in opting for a 'different' career and in carrying through their conviction in the face of possible peer group pressure and parental dismay. Some will succumb to the option of achieving short-term status through motherhood even though, in year 10, young women seem determined to have a career: 'A lot of my sister's friends have got children – they're like 18 and that. They're tied down. They can't have a career.

I want to live my life first'. But for many, there is satisfaction in motherhood – as a teacher explained:

(Many of the young women here) lead deprived lives, emotionally and materially, a lot of them, so having your own baby and being a unit of two takes you away from that kind of battering or abusing or simply uncaring . . . people can't push you around, can't tell you what to do. You are a mother.

There is, also, as teachers recognise, a need to do more for male pupils in terms of their aspirations and achievements. As one female teacher said, 'Girls have caught on, you know, and they are seeing a new outlook on life or a different role for them'. Helping young men to think more positively and ambitiously about careers and to recognise that qualifications are an asset has, at the same time, to be complemented by ways of helping them to accept the changes in domestic role and responsibility that the local employment situation, for example, is dictating: one teacher noted that often when she passed the primary school in the morning, 'there are quite a few men pushing the push-chairs. The women have got work; they can get work easily, while the father's unemployed'. And several students commented that fathers were beginning to share cooking and other domestic work. But by no means all.

What the school can try to build is some sense of self-worth and determination among young women, and also give attention to increasing the aspiration of young male students. The school's intake has become increasingly disadvantaged in recent years and many families need their children to bring in a wage if and when they can. While there are many unemployed in the area, and staying-on rates might be expected to increase to reflect the central pattern, recent figures are still disappointing: in 1990, 17 per cent went into the sixth form and 11 per cent into FE – a total of only 28 per cent. Young school leavers are, in the main, still able to get some work or training of some kind. Clearly, as in many schools, teachers are aware that, for the work on equality to bear fruit in practical ways, fundamental changes are needed in local employment openings, in the attitudes of employers, as well as in family attitudes and practices. There are changes, and the question is, can we be sure that the trend will continue? The pupils themselves indicated the continuing problems in the workplace but also the beginnings of some different basis of sharing in the home:

(When I marry) we'd both have part time jobs and try and get the shifts
sorted out so he can look after the children as well. (year 10)

My mother thinks that men should do just as much things like housework
as women but my father thinks that it is like a woman's job and that he is
the breadwinner. (year 10)

My dad when my mum comes in from work, my dad normally puts the
dinner on and cleans up and that. (year 9)

Some pupils are also able to see that their perceptions are different from
those of their family and that change is happening. A sixth former
commented: 'I don't think my parents have got there yet'.

A dilemma for the school is whether to plan a programme of equal
opportunities activity for parents – recognising that there is no strong
tradition of attendance at school events – or merely accept that change
will only come very slowly, through beginning to liberate the attitudes
and aspirations of succeeding cohorts of students, many of whom,
in time, will be parents within this same community. The problem
with the second strategy is whether what the students learn in school
can actually be enacted given the constrained and conventional opportunities for employment locally and the continuing sources of peer
group pride and pressure outside the school.

A female deputy offered a realistic view of the situation, but remained
convinced that it was important that the school maintained the level
and quality of its efforts:

On equal opportunities, some of it will stay and affect the next generation
(but) I suspect that what actually remains once they leave the school building
is a small part, probably quite a small part, but we continue and we build
on it and I think that maybe when we get the children of the children we
are now teaching that little bit that's perhaps been left with the first parent
can be built on with their child. I think it's a very slow process.

Harry, the male deputy whose professional commitment to whole-
school change has sustained the initiative, is equally realistic:

We're getting a leavening. But it's a long term job. It's endless. It'll never
stop. We have an idea which we'll never achieve. And we'll never see the
fruits of what we're doing for, well, twenty odd years. Those of us here
now may have left. But the ones that don't want to be part of it will be isolated
by the gradual progression, and our determination. There will be jumps
forward and we will have bad times, but we have made it clear to everybody
that that's what we're about.

6 POLICY AND PROGRESS: GUIDELINES FOR ACTION

How do we judge the progress that schools make in relation to gender equality?

It is not easy, and there are several reasons why this is so. We have to recognise the complexity of what is being attempted – and acknowledge that the task will be more difficult in some contexts than in others. It will be difficult, for instance, in areas where there is no tradition of geographical mobility and where the labour market differentiates in conventional ways between jobs for girls and jobs for boys: where jobs are scarce, people are less likely to challenge the gendered basis of such differentiation. And in areas where communities support traditional sex roles and divisions of labour, and where there is competition for pupil numbers, schools may be reluctant to emphasise policies that the community will regard with suspicion – equal opportunities policies, for instance. Teachers who *do* work on gender equality in such circumstances will probably find the going tough, and, as in the current debate about league tables, to apply absolute criteria across schools would be unfair.

Nor is it a simple matter to think of evaluating progress in terms of long-term goals, such as the capacity of groups of pupils from particular schools to seek and sustain occupations and roles that break with gendered traditions. Outside and beyond schooling, the pressures on young people to conform would make it difficult to chart the effects of schooling on the life courses of former pupils – and the pressures would be impossible to control.

And in thinking about evaluating progress, we also have to bear in mind that schools will define different levels of aspiration for their work. This will be due, in part, to the fact that teachers' access to the debate about gender equality varies and is often restricted. Gender leaders have an important contribution to make in introducing a language and conceptual framework for thinking about and talking about equality issues.

And in considering whole-school approaches, we need to be properly sceptical. It would be unrealistic to expect to build uniform commitment across the diversity of individuals who make up a school staff. What may look like whole-school commitment will probably prove to be a substantial patch of agreement and active support but with some ragged corners. There may also be one or two of the 'old school' antis around – being interviewed by a researcher may even rekindle a few oppositional sparks! But they pose no threat for the majority of their colleagues who will probably regard them, now, as marginalised misfits, for the school has moved on and they know that this is so.

In trying to judge progress, we may have to be content with some softer approaches. For instance, in relation to the Townley School I tried to get some measure of the changes that had taken place by asking staff and older pupils to look back on how things were and talk about how things are now different. I also asked new staff – their previous schools served as some kind of yardstick – how they saw Townley School in relation to work on equality issues.

Alternatively we could identify some broad 'compliance criteria'. Instead of looking for hard evidence of impact, we would try, instead, to identify categories of possible action which experience, reason and research all suggest are supportive of the development of gender equality. We would then see to what extent schools *are* taking action.

Using this approach, it is possible to identify three levels of commitment which I shall call:

- the level of heightened individual awareness;
- the level of organisational coherence;
- the level of analytic coherence.

Let us look first at the level of heightened individual awareness. What might count as acceptable evidence at this level? Individual teachers might be doing most of the things on this list:

Guidelines for Classroom Teachers
- Examine the seating arrangements: are girls and boys seated separately? Is this their choice?
- Check whether lists are organised by gender, or alphabetically or chronologically.
- Check how tasks are allocated in mixed gender groups: who takes notes? Who is dominant?

- Check that boys and girls receive equal amounts of the teacher's time and attention.
- Be scrupulous about using non-sexist language in talking with, or about, pupils – including pupils in the class and people generally.
- Reflect on what particular qualities or achievements girls and boys are given praise for or are reprimanded for.
- Make sure that boys are not singled out to help with 'heavy' tasks and girls with 'caring' tasks.
- Look critically at the criteria used for assessing pupils' work, and the comments made by the teacher: are comments on neatness made only about girls' work? Are comments about imagination and energy made only about boys' work?
- Make sure that texts do not communicate stereotypical images of men and women or of particular occupations.
- Make sure that the content of lessons gives due recognition to women's activities and their contribution to knowledge in the field.

(The items in this list have been brought together from documents drawn up by schools and by the Centre for the Study of Comprehensive Schools (CSCS); the items are intended as examples and the list does not claim completeness.)

Lists such as this are widely available and may well be circulated to all members of staff within a department or school. If they are taken seriously and acted on then they will ensure good practice at the level of the individual classroom teacher. They will be more effective, however, if they are part of a set of concerns that carry through the implicit values and principles into a wider institutional arena, and if there is some acceptance of the need for institutional monitoring.

A second step would be to complement the guidelines for individual classroom teachers with guidelines which focus on action at the departmental level and at the level of heads of year. Here are some examples of items that might be found on such lists:

Guidelines for Heads of Department
- Make sure that the equal opportunities dimensions of items on the agenda of departmental meetings are always taken into account.
- Scrutinise departmental schemes of work to see if they encourage non-sexist approaches.
- Scrutinise new texts before purchase in order to check sexist/racist bias in content, language and images.
- Regularly check assessment data to see if there are significant

differences between the grades for girls and boys, and the reports made on the work of girls and boys.

- If your subject is a GCSE option, check the numbers of boys and girls who opt for it and the grades that are achieved.

- If work in your department involves pupils in outside visits, are you prepared to tackle sexist language or practices among those who host your pupils?

Guidelines for Heads of Year

- Think about the way assemblies are prepared and presented. Who leads them? What do they focus on? Are they of equal interest to girls and boys? Do they present positive images of girls and women?

- In any formal settings, check the seating arrangements for staff and pupils to see if these arrangements reflect assumptions about gender.

- Look at the way space is used in the school and outside: are boys dominating particular areas? Do girls colonise other spaces?

- Look critically at policy and practice in relation to uniform. Is the uniform restrictive in any way to either sex? Do rules apply equally to girls and boys?

- What assumptions are made about pupils who need special help. For instance, does most support go to disruptive boys? What about girls who may demonstrate their resistance or disaffection more quietly?

- Look at extra-curricular activities. Does the gender of the teacher leading a particular activity reflect traditional stereotypes? Are the interests and needs of girls and boys catered for equally well?

Guidelines addressed specifically to the members of the senior management team would emphasise a commitment to collecting and analysing, on a regular basis, certain kinds of information (about assessment, options and destinations, for example). They would also outline a strategy for monitoring progress on the various fronts. They would guarantee that the existing responsibility structure would be looked at in terms of gendered inequalities, and they would suggest a strategy for fostering commitment to non-sexist practices among all staff. Such documents might be part of, or linked to, a policy statement which justifies the school's prioritising of equal opportunities.

The aspirations and concerns expressed in such practices would take a school onto the second level of commitment – *the level of organisational coherence*. This level is characterised by three qualities: coverage, courage and consistency. Coverage is about looking steadily and with determination across the various areas of institutional responsibility, including some – promotions, hierarchies, dealing with sexual harassment, for instance – that are, in many settings, bound to be sensitive. Courage is about a readiness to be up front, direct and clear about values, to be able to justify those values, and to be prepared to stand by them. Consistency is about establishing a framework of concern and watchfulness within which all staff and all pupils are expected to act. It means monitoring behaviour and being prepared to use appropriate sanctions. It means monitoring progress. And it means reviewing goals and any written guidelines since these may need extending or refocusing as a school's understanding of the practical significance of gender equality develops.

To summarise: the following items would count as evidence that a school was working at this level of commitment:

- There is (or the school is working towards) a policy statement that expresses commitment to equality, that is clear in intent and that all members of the school know is to be taken seriously. This policy statement may be supplemented by documents that offer clear, practical guidelines to classroom teachers, to heads of department, to year heads and to the senior management team.
- The school has a system for monitoring adherence to the principles expressed in its policy statement. Its strategies for dealing with problems will be firm and fair – and yet not without understanding of the difficulties individuals have, in our society, in translating equality principles into practice on a daily basis.
- The school has a system for maintaining records that enable it to analyse data along equality dimensions. There is an expectation that the analyses will be discussed within the school, and that, where necessary, action will be taken.
- Advertisements for posts within the school (or the 'further information available') will emphasise the school's commitment to equality issues so that staff who apply know that equality is a central concern of the school, and so that the appointing panel can be confident that the person appointed will respect and actively endorse the values and principles that the school stands by.
- The school is concerned that all its members – including ancillary and support staff – understand what the principles mean for their work in the school.
- The school is prepared to find ways of sharing its values and principles with groups and individuals who regularly relate to pupils (including parents) or who work with pupils on particular occasions (such as employers involved in work experience or other school-industry schemes).

No school could realistically meet these criteria if the head and senior management team were not genuinely and fully committed to principles of equality. As the accounts in earlier chapters suggest, the support of senior staff is vital to the effective development of a whole-school equality policy. Beyond this, there is a third level of commitment, that of *analytic coherence*. In order to explain what I mean by this I shall have to step back for a moment.

Across the country, there has undoubtedly been a change in the level of general awareness of gender issues. Language patterns reflect this change. There are visibly more women in senior positions in industry, in education, in politics – although the number as a proportion of all senior positions is still very small. The popular media are reflecting a new tolerance of women in what were, hitherto, exclusively male domains – although the tolerance of the general public may be limited to 'life on the box'. Nevertheless, women are seen making successful careers as comedians, for example, and audiences have been prepared to watch programmes featuring female managers of a football team or successful business women. Of course, these changes may signify little more than the melting tip of the iceberg of female disadvantage; the bulk may yet remain invisible and frozen. Or they may be the small beginnings of a long revolution.

Schools are playing their part. As Hargeaves (1982: 185) has said, 'education cannot directly and of itself produce an end to inequalities'. 'But', he goes on:

> an acceptance of that proposition does not entail a denial that education could exercise an important and unique role in the process of social amelioration . . . To that end . . . we must design a secondary education with more self-conscious social and political objectives. Otherwise the school will continue to act as a conservative force, reflecting and confirming the status quo rather than generating the will and the skill through which we can make a better society.

'Analytic coherence' has something to do with the defining of 'more self-conscious social and political objectives': it is about recognising something of the social and economic foundations of gender inequalities. It means looking beyond the short-term successes and understanding the tight weave of the structures that hold inequality in place. Such understanding is not easy to achieve.

We have seen in the past what happens to innovations that are 'accepted' into a school under pressure; in such circumstances implementation may amount to little more than a superficial, unthinking conformity. Fundamental change – that is, change that affects the deeper structures of our thinking and action – needs to be understood and made our own. There are of course different ways of building such an understanding. One route is through history – becoming familiar, for instance, with the politicisation of notions of equality since the 1944 Education Act; or with the direction taken by the equality of opportunity debate – starting, perhaps, with Coleman and colleagues' study in the US in the 1960s, which argued that 'academic performance was determined almost entirely by background characteristics of students' (Chubb and Moe 1990: 14) and following it through to recent research which claims that schools *do* make a difference. Another way would be to follow the contours of the controversy about working within a framework that emphasises 'equality of opportunity' as opposed to one that emphasises 'equality of outcome'. Or one might try to see whether, in relation to the local community, Sultana (1990: 20) is right in saying that young people's 'pre-existing gender identities become transferred into male advantage and female disadvantage', or, alternatively, whether Arnot (1991: 453) is right in suggesting that although girls learn 'to express non-traditional attitudes about male and female roles in society', they tend not to change their behaviour when it comes to 'making educational or occupational choices'. These are some of the issues which teachers committed to gender equality have found it useful to examine in order to get a more profound sense of what schools can effectively do to support the cause of gender equality in our society.

One distinctive feature of most of the 'gender leaders' who were interviewed in the present study was that they had read about and debated these issues – but not, generally, with their own colleagues in their own schools: discussions had taken place at meetings of regional or national gender networks, or in MEd/MA programmes where there were women's studies units or single options on gender equality. Given the pressures on teachers during the school day it is not surprising that the school is not a site for reflective discourse about fundamental educational issues – and what little space there may be is currently being used for debates about the new curricular structures and programmes of testing. And organisers of the occasional whole-school staff development days often feel obliged to put on events which are more actively 'training' oriented than reflection oriented.

It is not easy, therefore, to see how the interested majority on a school staff might together move onto this third level of commitment, and achieve analytic awareness which is the foundation for 'analytic coherence'. But it is important. The quality of analytic coherence is what gives substance and dynamic integrity to fragmented ideas and practices. It helps in defining priorities and in thinking through the nature of a school's responsibility to its own pupils, to the community, and to society. It could also help teachers think about evaluating progress on gender equality: are they aiming at improvement within the boundaries of the school's sphere of influence, or do they see themselves as contributing to a much slower and broader process of social change – or both? And they might take as their overarching question the one posed by Mimi Orner (1992: 85):

How can we present and explore identity and difference not as instruments of division but as unifying forces?

7 INDIVIDUALS AND INSTITUTIONS: THE DILEMMAS OF CHANGE

Never was a walk so calmly
   undertaken.
Past the waiting WI,
   flower-of-the-month in hand,
   clear-headed, light-footed,
   with an almost religious fervour,
   as if to an unseen shrine.
Escaping to the high road,
   ripe with meadowsweet
   and agricultural smells.
Out of the farmlands;
   out of matrimony.
            (Rosemary Burnett 1991: 2)

This poem captures, in a few lines, the courage and determination needed for an individual to undo the ties that bind her, or him, to a social institution. In this case it is a woman leaving a marriage but it is also about the edifice of expectations that hold people back. The opening hints at the turmoil of guilt and doubt that preceded the moment of decision. The walk is the culmination of a process in which the woman sought understanding of her situation and found the strength to act.

This experience is mirrored in the stories that many of the people I interviewed told me. The settings are different; the events themselves not so momentous, perhaps – but the feelings are recognisable. Carrie, for instance, was irritated by the way that science comes to be seen 'as a subject that enhances masculinity' so that girls 'back off' as they get older and boys fill the space, engaging the teacher in excited dialogue. She had to acknowledge, to her dismay, that she enjoyed teaching the boys more than she did the girls. Carrie reflected on her reactions and decided to change the structure of the situation:

I have taken a deep breath and done something really quite dramatic with a particular group. I laid down the law for one lesson and I said that no boy was to approach me for any assistance whatsoever. I said that I would choose who I would work with. Nobody must track a path to me. I made this clear to the boys and I explained why. And I made a profound discovery: when you have the nerve actually to do it, and you believe in it enough, it works. The boys – including the really dominant ones in the group – sorted themselves out and got on. I had tried to do something like it earlier but I'd been more feeble-minded about it and I'd introduced it almost surreptitiously and my worst fears were realised – the boys upped the stakes in attention-seeking behaviour. This time I was very clear about what I was going to do and somehow my body language, my eyes, everything communicated that this was going to happen. And it did. You need that sort of commitment to change. You need to believe that change *must* happen and *is* possible.

Over a period of time, Carrie had analysed a recurrent situation, had decided that intervention was justifiable, and had walked away, with determination, from the habits that had sustained the disparities that troubled her. She reflected on her capacity to do this: 'You have to be a very confident woman to be prepared to model an alternative way to students and to staff.' Her confidence had grown out of personal struggle and the anger she felt 'about the power relationships that operate' in the institution of schooling.

Developing a gender policy in schools is particularly difficult. As Davies (1989: 229) says, gender is created by individuals and within individuals 'as they learn what it is to be male or female, and through which they become locked into [and thus limited by] masculine and feminine subject positions'. By the time pupils arrive in school they have 'already acquired a personal baggage' (p. 239) that affects the way they look at things and their freedom of choice. Most teachers bring a similar baggage with them. The school as an institution tends to reinforce, through its structures and assumptions, the parameters of gender identity:

It is not easy to overcome . . . years of gender socialisation on the part of pupils, nor the allegiance of some of the staff to a society organised by gender.

(Woods 1990: 81)

Davies (1989: 230–31) writes memorably about the reactions of pre-school children to a story she read them. Princess Elizabeth and Prince Ronald are planning to get married but a dragon comes along, burns Elizabeth's castle and possessions, and carries off Ronald. Elizabeth is angry and, soot-covered from the fire and dressed only in a paper bag, she sets off to rescue Ronald. He tells her that he doesn't want to be saved by a woman who looks so scruffy. 'Come back when you look like a real Princess', he says. Elizabeth is taken aback but replies, with spirit: 'You may look like a real Prince, but you're a bum'. The last page shows her skipping off into the sunset alone and the story ends with the words: 'They didn't get married after all'. Davies comments: 'Many of the children to whom I read this story were unable to see Elizabeth as a genuine hero' and were not sympathetic to her decision to go it alone: 'Most children believed Elizabeth should have cleaned herself up and then married the Prince'.

This is a nice example of the 'baggage' – the predispositions and patterns of expectation – that children bring with them into school. Because as adults we are already so familiar with our own ways of thinking and those of others, we find it difficult to 'see' how we are structuring the world and our own position in it. Rosemary Burnett (1991: 10) reminds us:

> Centuries of tradition,
>   coupled with
>   my mother's own example,
>   instilled
>   an anxiety to please,
>   to abase myself;
>   subordinate ambition
>   for expediency.
> And how the biological bit,
>   that joker in the pack of thieves,
>   s-t-r-e-t-c-h-e-d out the scenario,
>   putting me down
>   in the missionary position
>   of pious acquiescence!
> More shameful to admit,
>   the aforesaid biological bit
>   actually wallowed in its stereotype.

There is a lot to undo, both at the level of the individual and at the level of the school. And undoing habits, taking away the paths we are used to walking down, leaves us feeling disoriented and vulnerable.

Building a whole-school gender policy is bound to breed discomfort: individuals face the possible unravelling and remaking of aspects of their personal world as well as the professional world they inhabit. And during the extensive period of transition, which marks all processes of cultural change, contradictions pull people and institutions in different directions. The different settings that we find ourselves in are all changing at a different pace – and there is bound to be some disorientation and apprehension. As Shilling (1991: 41) explains: 'Because schools are just one locale (or set of locales) among many others in society, those in them face a difficult task in altering rules and resources which remain unchallenged in other centrally important areas of social life'.

Anyon's work is helpful here. She describes what it is like to find yourself receiving conflicting messages about gender; part of all human beings' response to such contradictions, she says, is a dialectic of accommodation and resistance (1983: 19; see also David 1991: 444). Let us look at some of these contradictions. Several women I talked with acknowledged the tension of maintaining a 'liberated woman' persona in the workplace and returning home to appear in the traditional roles that their family expected of them. They may experience what Anyon (1983: 24) describes as 'an internal resistance; a separateness; an internal non-subordination'. They would like, they say, greater unity in their lives, bringing their domestic image closer to their professional image, but as Claire Duchen has said: 'the tailoring of desire to the logic of politics is not always possible' (quoted by Rowbotham, 1989). Other women talked about the discrepancy between their public facade of support for equality and their private doubts: at heart they suspected that they continued to accept the ideologies that devalue women. They may be struggling to understand the basis of their own achievement: 'I've made it as a single mother and a working woman and I didn't have any of this equal opps stuff, so why can't others?' Or they may be trying to protect their own children from the discomfort of being different from their peers.

In a study of primary school teachers, Evans (1982, cited by Acker 1988: 314) describes the contradictions between the desire to identify with traditional gender roles and images of femininity and the desire to compete, as career women, for equality with men. Jean Anyon tracks these contradictions into the homes of working class women: 'The charge of femininity – to be submissive, subordinate to their men, dependent and domestic – is in sharp dysjunction with the imperatives of their daily lives – the need, for example, to struggle aggressively for survival' (1983: 20). Evans nicely captures the condition which many women find themselves in in her phrase, the 'ambiguity of self'. Interestingly, the women who talked autobiographically (see Chapter 2) about the shaping of their commitment to gender equality looked back on critical events in their lives – separation, for instance – as occasions which created space, untied some of the threads of uncertainty and dependence, and allowed them to reflect on their identities and aspirations.

Contradictions are also experienced by young people in school. While their school may offer female pupils strong messages about continuing their education and aspiring to a career, the peer culture continues to suggest, in many settings, that a woman's self-esteem and survival depend on finding and holding a man as partner, with the result that identity, as Lynn Davies (1983: 41) suggests, is shaped largely through how others – teachers, parents, boyfriends – treat you. In this way, the cycle of subordination is perpetuated. Indeed, there is evidence that stereotyping of academically inclined pupils and non-academically inclined pupils by appearance has not died out. David Gillborn (1990: 171), for example, recalls a remark made by a teacher about a tall bespectacled girl: 'She's a bright girl, she is . . . She looks it though, doesn't she?' Gillborn comments: 'I do not wish to imply that . . . every girl who seemed in any way "attractive" was automatically assumed to be stupid. Rather, I would state that a concern with what many male staff saw as "feminine preoccupations" (e.g. cosmetics and fashion) may . . . act against the image of [a] pupil as someone who took education seriously'. This is one of what Lynn Davies calls 'the official typescripts' that are still available for females.

Magda Lewis writes strongly about such dilemmas (1992: 182–3), including those facing young lesbians in schools where sexuality and sexual orientation are not openly discussed (see also Mac an Ghaill 1991; Kelly 1992). But there are also the dilemmas facing lesbian teachers: those who 'do not comply, at least nominally, with acceptable standards of self-presentation do not escape the consequences of marginalisation and exclusion.' She concludes that for all women in professional settings (and in some domestic settings also), 'compliance with particular displays of femininity' are central to the expectations that accompany the job. Those who step outside the norms are likely to find how ridicule is used as a particularly effective form of social control (see Acker 1988: 318; Squirrell 1989).

Equal opportunities initiatives do not, in the short-term, help resolve the contradictions that touch the lives of young women in schools and their teachers; they serve to expose them so that they can be explored. And, as Liz Kelly suggests, it is precisely this recognition, that such contradictions and dilemmas 'are present in our daily lives and experiences' that defines, in part, 'a feminist perspective' (1992: 33).

We have also to realise that the structuring of these contradictions reflects the playing out of larger forces on the national stage. Madeleine Arnot (1992) reminds us of the implicit promise of women's liberation in the 1944 Education Act and the ironies of neglect that have left the aspiration only partially realised. She quotes Rowbotham (1986: 85) who says that the expansion of education 'hurtled a generation of women beyond the confines of their mothers' world into the male sphere of public affairs and work' – only to find that no provision had been made for childcare. There were growing tensions between the plots that tied women into their 'domestic destinies' and the scripts written for their entry into the labour market. And in the 1980s according to ten Tusscher (1986: 76; quoted by Arnot, 1992: 54), the New Right was committed to 'the twin goals of restoring class forces in favour of capital and of restoring gender relations in favour of men'. In 1988, 44 years after the first major commitment to equality, we had the Education Reform Act but it has not allayed our anxieties. According to the growing number of feminist critiques, the promise of an entitlement curriculum masks the subtle workings of Margaret Thatcher's (the then prime minister's) commitment to the status quo of gender relations – as expressed in her vigorous promotion of the image of the family and of Victorian values. With so little help from the new education reforms, the responsibility for taking gender seriously is left largely to individual schools.

Gendered inequalities cannot easily be combated unless the structures that sustain them are understood – hence the emphasis in the last chapter on the capacity for analytic consciousness. We need to see, in schools, how the scaffolding of gendered assumptions and practices makes institutional change difficult, as well as the contradictions that individuals experience as they encounter the conflicting messages of a society in flux. And we need to be sympathetic to the task of change as well as determined to pursue it.

To the teachers whose work in schools I have tried to document – both women and men – I want to say (echoing the words Jeanette Winterson took from The Medea, 1987) that you have not reached the end of the journey but the progress you have made in the most difficult of climates and circumstances is impressive:

> You have navigated well, passing beyond the sea's double rocks and ranging far from the paternal home.

REFERENCES

Acker, S. (1988) Teachers, gender and resistance, *British Journal of Sociology of Education*, 9(3), 307–22.

Anyon, J. (1983) Intersections of gender and class: accommodation and resistance by working class and affluent females to contradictory sex-role ideologies. In S. Walker and L. Barton (eds) *Gender, Class and Education*, Lewes: Falmer Press.

Arnot, M. (1989) Crisis or challenge; equal opportunities in the national curriculum, *NUT Education Review*, 3(2), 7–14.

Arnot, M. (1991) Equality and democracy: a decade of struggle over education, *British Journal of Sociology of Education*, 12(4), 447–66.

Arnot, M. (1992) Feminism, education and the new right. In M. Arnot and L. Barton (eds) *Voicing Concerns: Sociological Perspectives on Contemporary Education Reforms*, Wallingford: Triangle Press.

Ball, S. (1987) *The Micro-Politics of the School*, London: Methuen.

Berger, J. (1992) *Keeping a Rendezvous*, London: Granta Books.

Bruner, J. (1986) *Actual Minds, Possible Worlds*, New York: Harvard University Press.

Burnett, R. (1991) *Points of Departure*, Minehead: The Nomads Press.

Chubb, J.E. and Moe, T.M. (1990) *Politics, Markets and America's Schools*, Washington: The Brookings Institute.

Coleman, J.S., Campbell, E.A., Hobson, C.J. *et al.* (1966) *Equality of Educational Opportunity* (the Coleman Report), Washington: US Government Printing Office.

Connel, R.W. (1987; reprinted 1991) *Gender and Power*, Oxford: Blackwell.

Connell, R.W., Ashenden, D.J., Kessler, S. and Dowsett, G.W. (1982) *Making the Difference*, Sydney: George Allen and Unwin.

Corson, D.J. (1992) Language, gender and education: a critical review linking social justice and power, *Gender and Education*, 4(3), 229–54.

CSCS (1990) *Gender Equality in Schools*, Leaflet no. 27, Leicester: Centre for the Study of Comprehensive Schools.

David, M. (1991) A gender agenda: women and family in the new ERA?, *British Journal of Sociology of Education*, 12(4), 433–46.

Davies, B. (1989) The discursive production of the male/female dualism in school settings, *Oxford Review of Education*, 15(3), 229–65.

Davies, L. (1983) Gender, resistance and power. In S. Walker and L. Barton (eds) *Gender, Class and Education*, Lewes: Falmer Press.

Evans, T. (1982) Being and becoming: teachers' perceptions of sex roles and actions towards their male and female pupils, *British Journal of Sociology of Education*, 3(2), 127–43.

Fine, M. and Gordon, S.M. (1991) Effacing the center and the margins, *Feminism and Psychology*, 1(1), 19–25.

Gillborn, D. (1990) Sexism and curricular 'choice', *Cambridge Journal of Education*, 20(2), 161–74.

Gillborn, D. (forthcoming) *Rethinking 'Race': The Politics of 'Race' in Education Research, Policy and Practice*, Buckingham: Open University Press.

Giroux, H.A. (1983) *Theory and Resistance in Education*, London: Heinemann Educational.

Greene, M. (1985) Teacher as project: choice, perspective and the public space, mimeo.

Hargreaves, D.H. (1982) *The Challenge for the Comprehensive School*, London: Routledge and Kegan Paul.

Hargreaves, D.H. (1989) Educational policy and educational change: a local perspective. In A. Hargreaves and D. Reynolds (eds) *Education Policies: Controversies and Critiques*, Lewes: Falmer Press.

Harris, S., Nixon, J. and Rudduck, J. (1993) Schoolwork, homework and gender, *Gender and Education*, 5(1), 3–15.

Huberman, M. (1989) Teacher development and instructed mastery. Paper given at the International Conference on Teacher Development: Policies, Practices and Research, OISE, Ontario.

Kelly, A. (1985) The construction of masculine science, *British Journal of Sociology of Education*, 6(2), 133–54.

Kelly, A. (1988) Gender differences in teacher-pupil interactions: a meta-analytic review, *Research in Education*, (39), 1–23.

Kelly, L. (1992) Not in front of the children: responding to right-wing agendas on sexuality and education. In M. Arnot and L. Barton (eds) *Voicing Concerns: Sociological Perspectives on Contemporary Education Reform*, Wallingford: Triangle Books.

Kenway, J. and Modra, H. (1992) Feminist pedagogy and emancipatory possibilities. In C. Luke and J. Gore (eds) *Feminisms and Critical Pedagogy*, London: Routledge.

Kessler, S., Ashenden, D.J., Connell, R.W. and Dowsett, G.W. (1985) Gender relations in secondary schooling, *Sociology of Education*, 58(1), 34–48.

Lather, P. (1992) Post-critical pedagogies: a feminist reading. In C. Luke and J. Gore (eds) *Feminisms and Critical Pedagogy*, London: Routledge.

Lewis, M. (1992) Interrupting patriarchy: politics, resistance and transformation in the feminist classroom. In C. Luke and J. Gore (eds) *Feminisms and Critical Pedagogy*, London: Routledge.

Mac an Ghaill, M. (1991) Schooling, sexuality and male power: towards an emancipatory curriculum, *Gender and Education*, 3(3), 291–309.

Meis, M. (1983) Towards a methodology of feminist research. In G. Bowles and R. Duelli Klein (eds) *Theories of Women's Studies*, London: Routledge and Kegan Paul.

Nias, J. (1984) Learning and acting the roles: in-school support for primary teachers, *Educational Review*, 36(1), 3–15.

Nixon, J. (forthcoming) *Encouraging Learning in Secondary Schools*, Buckingham: Open University Press.

Orner, M. (1992) Interrupting the calls for student voice in 'liberatory' education: a feminist poststructuralist perspective. In C. Luke and J. Gore (eds) *Feminisms and Critical Pedagogy*, London: Routledge.

Orr, P. (1985) Sex bias in schools: national perspectives. In J. Whyte, R. Deem, L. Kant and M. Cruikshank (eds) *Girl Friendly Schooling*, London: Routledge.

Ortega y Gasset, J. (1984) *Historical Reason*, New York: W.W. Norton.

Polanyi, M. (1958) *Personal Knowledge*, London: Routledge and Kegan Paul.

Reynolds, D. (1984) Relative autonomy reconstructed. In L. Barton and S. Walker (eds) *Social Crisis in Educational Research*, London: Croom Helm.

Reynolds, D. and Packer, A. (1992) School effectiveness and school improvement. In D. Reynolds and P. Cuttance (eds) *School Effectiveness: Research, Policy and Practice*, London: Cassell.

Riddell, S.I. (1992) *Gender and the Politics of the Curriculum*, London: Routledge.

Rowbotham, S. (1986) Feminism and democracy. In D. Held and C. Pollitt (eds) *New Forms of Democracy*, London: Sage Books.

Rowbotham, S. (1989) To be or not to be: the dilemmas of mothering, *Feminist Review*, (31), 82–93.

Rudduck, J. (1991) *Innovation and Change*, Buckingham: Open University Press.

Shilling, C. (1991) Social space, gender inequalities and educational differentiation, *British Journal of Sociology of Education*, 12(1), 23–44.

Skeggs, B. (1992) The constraints of neutrality: ERA and feminist research. Paper given at an ESRC seminar, University of Warwick, November.

Skelton, C. and Hanson, J. (1989) Schooling the teachers: gender and initial teacher education. In S. Acker (ed.) *Teachers, Gender and Careers*, Lewes: Falmer Press.

Smyth, J. (1987) Transforming teaching through intellectualising the work of teachers. In J. Smyth (ed.) *Educating Teachers*, Lewes: Falmer Press.

Squirrell, G. (1989) In passing . . . teachers and sexual orientation. In S. Acker (ed.) *Teachers, Gender and Careers*, Lewes: Falmer Press.

Stanley, L. and Wise, S. (1983) *Breaking Out: Feminist Consciousness and Feminist Research*, London: Routledge and Kegan Paul.

Sultana, R.G. (1990) Gender, schooling and transformation, *New Zealand Journal of Educational Studies*, 25(1), 5–25.

ten Tusscher, T. (1986) Patriarchy, capitalism and the new right. In J. Evans, J. Hills, K. Hunt *et al.* (eds) *Feminism and Political Theory*, London: Sage.

Weiner, G. (1985) Equal opportunities, feminism and girls' education. In G. Weiner (ed.) *Just a Bunch of Girls*, Milton Keynes: Open University Press.

Weiner, G. (1986) Feminist education and equal opportunities: unity or discord?, *British Journal of Sociology of Education*, 7(3), 265–274.

Whyld, J. (ed.) (1983) *Sexism in the Secondary School*, London: Harper and Row.

Whyte, J. (1986) *Girls into Science and Technology: The Story of a Project*, London: Routledge and Kegan Paul.

Wilson, E. (1980) *Only Halfpenny to Paradise: Women in Britain*, London: Tavistock.

Winterson, J. (1987) *The Passion*, Harmondsworth: Penguin Books.

Woods, P. (1990) *The Happiest Days? How Pupils Cope with School*, Lewes: Falmer Press.

Wright, C. (1987) The relations between teachers and Afro-Caribbean pupils: observing multi-racial classrooms. In G. Weiner and M. Arnot (eds) *Gender under Scrutiny*, London: Hutchinson.

NAME INDEX

GENERAL INDEX

GENDER PLAY
GIRLS AND BOYS IN SCHOOL
Barrie Thorne

You see it in every school playground: the girls play only with girls, the boys play only with boys. Why? And what do the children themselves think about this? Breaking with familiar conventions for thinking about children and gender, *Gender Play* develops fresh insights into the everyday social worlds of kids in schools. Barrie Thorne draws on her daily observations in the classroom and on the playground to show how children construct and experience gender in school. With rich detail she looks at the 'play of gender' in the organization of groups of children and activities. Thorne argues that the organization and meaning of gender are influenced by age, ethnicity, race, sexuality, and social class and that they shift with social context. She sees gender identity not through the lens of individual socialization or difference, but rather as a social process involving groups of children. Thorne takes us on a fascinating journey of discovery, provides new insights into the behaviour of children, and offers teachers practical suggestions for increasing cooperative, mixed-gender interaction.

> A stunning achievement . . . Thorne transforms our ability to see gender in social life. She demonstrates that every action . . . is worthy of interpretation and infused with social and cultural meaning . . . Feminist scholarship takes a major step forward with this book.
> (Nancy J. Chodorow, author of *Feminism and Psychoanalytic Theory*)

> This is a beautifully observed, as well as deeply reflective book . . . Pathbreaking research is combined with vivid and enjoyable writing. Thorne will help teachers and parents, as well as students and researchers, gain a new understanding of issues about gender.
> (Bob Connell, author of *Gender and Power*)

Contents
Children and gender – learning from kids – Boys and girls together . . . but mostly apart – Gender separation: why and how – Creating a sense of 'opposite sides' – Do girls and boys have different cultures? – Crossing the gender divide – Lip gloss and 'goin' with': becoming teens – Lessons for adults – Notes – References – Index.

252pp   0 335 19123 1 (Paperback)

MARKS ON THE MEMORY
EXPERIENCING SCHOOL

Julia Stanley

This is an original account of six 'ordinary' teenagers coming to the end of their compulsory schooling. Julia Stanley 'lived' with them in school for two years, and we come to know their lives, homes, teachers and futures through her eyes *and* theirs. A number of issues arose naturally from daily life in the school, including:

- Why did fourth and fifth year pupils persevere with examinations designed to fail 40 per cent of them?
- How do individuals cope with big secondary schools, and do they adapt through a 'personal curriculum'?
- How do girls and boys differ in their ways of coping?
- How far is the school part of the community, and in touch with local public opinion?

The book is innovatory because it takes stock of comprehensive schooling at a turning point in its history, and because it is a 'democratic ethnography' in which the young people and their families were encouraged to contribute to the conclusion. Above all, however, this is the fascinating story of how six 'normal' teenagers adapt to the social and educational demands of life in an 'average' state school. We experience what it really feels like to be a pupil in a modern comprehensive.

Contents
4T's home town – Why Gregory went to school – Salt of the earth – How not to do it – A better class of person – Speaking your mind – Tracy Shore learns to go through life – The art of being nobody – The legacy of the past – Equal opportunities and the educational vacuum – Where do we go from here? – Appendix – Index.

192pp   0 335 09557 7 (Paperback)   0 335 09558 5 (Hardback)

WHAT'S WORTH FIGHTING FOR IN YOUR SCHOOL?
WORKING TOGETHER FOR IMPROVEMENT

Michael Fullan and Andy Hargreaves

This is about how to make schools more interesting and fulfilling places to be. It tackles how to bring about marked improvements in the daily lives and experiences of teachers, heads and pupils. The premise is that teachers and heads themselves should ultimately *make* this happen.

Almost everywhere, teachers and heads are overloaded and undervalued. Teachers and heads will need to take more of the initiative themselves, not just in holding off unreasonable demands, not just in bargaining for better conditions but also in making constructive improvements of their own, as a professional community. Examples of such constructive practice already exist but they need to be broadened, strengthened and developed. This book is meant to stimulate such improvements. It is a practical book and a provocative one; fully aware of the constraints and everyday problems facing teachers but clear in setting out what really is worth fighting for in schools.

No teacher or head will read this book without responding in the light of his or her personal experiences, beliefs and passion about teaching; and all will be challenged by this catalyst for action.

Contents

160pp   0 335 15755 6 (Paperback)